HEY, PROFESSOR

HEY, PROFESSOR

An Experiment
in Distance Learning and Teaching
by a College English Department Instructor
and 27 Sheltered-in-Place New York City
Undergraduate Students
Enrolled in a Humanities Course
Studying, of All Things, the Literature of Waiting

ROBERT EIDELBERG

To order additional copies of this book, contact:
Xlibris
1-888-795-4274
www.Xlibris.com
Orders@Xlibris.com
815307

NOT SO MUCH CHAPTERS IN THIS BOOK AS 27 ON-CAMPUS AND DISTANCE-LEARNER PORTRAITS OF REMOTE LIVES IN THE LAND OF EMAILED EDUCATION

NOT EVEN REMOTELY THIS BOOK'S DEDICATION PAGE BUT, INSTEAD, TODAY'S SURPRISE TRUE OR FALSE QUIZ ON, WHO WOULD HAVE THOUGHT: DISTANCE LEARNING

So, True or False, Distance Learning Is:

- ✓ the non-pandemic wave of the future in college education
- ✓ the long-time-coming death blow to a liberal arts education
- ✓ the solution to the problem of finding, affording, and holding on to quality college professors
- ✓ the best thing to happen to charismatic teaching since Socrates
- ✓ the diversification and democratization of a university's student body
- ✓ an indirect symbol of white wealth and privilege
- ✓ a demonstrable reason for partial remission of tuition
- ✓ technically impossible for talented Luddites
- ✓ an innovation in professorial pedagogy
- ✓ supremely cost effective
- ✓ not even remotely humanistic instruction
- ✓ favored by most undergraduates
- ✓ a hiring opportunity for local teaching assistants
- ✓ the end of stimulating discussion-based courses
- ✓ a financial bonanza for ed-tech companies and their stockholders
- ✓ a cost-saving approach that will save many small colleges from going bankrupt
- ✓ the end of the intimate classroom, the physical campus, and mentoring
- ✓ really "distant" learning, as in the learning that is quite far away from the here and the now
- ✓ the revitalization of the lecture approach to instruction
- ✓ the end of joy in being a teacher
- ✓ like teaching into outer space where learning cannot be read on the faces of students
- ✓ the death of intelligence other than artificial
- ✓ an assumption of equity among students learning remotely
- ✓ the final silencing of E.M. Forster's "only connect"
- ✓ the start of a great tuning out by poor and minority students

- ✓ the end of the school building as an equalizer
- ✓ teaching as tech support
- ✓ the first step in ending student debt
- ✓ the degrading of the value of a college education
- ✓ not good for an individual's mental health and for family cohesion
- ✓ passive, with the potential for passive aggressive
- ✓ the end of the small class size movement
- ✓ the end of middle-class campus life
- ✓ the enrichment of the top quality universities
- ✓ the homogenization and standardization of content
- ✓ the triumph of knowledge over understanding
- ✓ the death of curiosity
- ✓ the devaluing of a college degree
- ✓ the saving of the importance of college certification for jobs
- ✓ the debasement of the intellectual
- ✓ the triumph of democracy over oligarchy
- ✓ a good start on overcoming classroom distractions
- ✓ the intensification of at-home distractions
- ✓ a further implementation of learn at your own pace
- ✓ the triumph of collegial competition in the classroom over challenge-based collaboration
- ✓ the end to learning-by-teaching-others
- ✓ the diminishment of the kind of education that takes place in college libraries, hallways, cafeterias, clubs
- ✓ a worsening of existing social inequalities
- ✓ a plus for the self-directed
- ✓ a slap at those with special needs and language disabilities
- ✓ a friend only to those with computers, laptops, and access to the internet

And the correct answers to this surprise true or false quiz?

Our 27 Hunter College undergraduate students (from Henry to Shanya) will let you know what they think they are – and then you can decide for yourself by the end of HEY, PROFESSOR: An Experiment in Distance Learning.

"Don't plan too carefully for your next mistake"
– the pedagogical mantra of a mentoring colleague

INTRODUCTION TO HEY, PROFESSOR

I knew three of them from before – in the way teachers know former students from their classroom participation and their written homeworks. There was college junior Shanya, whom I had given an A+ to just last term in my special topics course on "The Teacher and Student in Literature," as well as Patrick and Valeria from that same Hunter College English Department course who had each earned an "A." Actually, I had come to know these three young people a bit more through our course's unique "one more thing" email, where students would write me those thoughts they hadn't gotten around to saying in class either because so many other students' hands had been up in the air to be called on or because they hadn't had a particular insight until they found themselves thinking about our Manhattan campus's classroom discussion on the subway ride home to one of the outer boroughs of New York City later that night.

I also sort of knew two others. There was Henry, a sophomore philosophy major who had sneaked into one of the final sessions last fall of "The Teacher and Student in Literature" to see whether I measured up to his high standards for the teaching of philosophical literature because he was interested in taking this brand-new special topics course of mine on "The Literature of Waiting" but wasn't going to trust my rather good reviews on the nationwide "www.ratemyprofessors.com" website.

And there was Christina, a senior I didn't know at all except from her email of a few days before the start of the spring 2020 term telling me she would be definitely missing the first class session of the course on the evening of January 28, and possibly the second meeting, because she was snowed in at a Lunar Day family gathering in upstate New York outside of Buffalo.

As for the rest of the class of 30 (ranging from upper freshmen to graduating seniors, and including one senior citizen auditor) that filled "The Literature of Waiting," well, how deeply I would know them I would have to wait, and see, and listen. But *exactly how* I would know them, well, that dramatically changed at almost the mid-point of the course on March 12 when, because of the elimination of any on-campus instruction at Hunter College and its fellow campuses that make up The City University of New York, my students and I gave control over to "the remote" and went off-campus and online.

Being a bit of a Luddite (a rather big bit, my students will tell you), I zero-ed out on using Zoom with its limited teacher-to-student interaction and pretty much non-existent student-to student interaction. Consequently, for the entire second half of my course, all teaching and learning in "The Literature of Waiting" was conducted through my online Blackboard announcements and assignments and by back-and-forth emailing between the students and me. (Since the class had already been divided into five groups containing six "groupmates" for an independent reading and oral presentation project, I expanded the number of assignments and activities that would require groupmates to share their written work and feedback thoughts, via email, to one another – and to me.)

But, in reality, what was formerly "one more thing" emails were about to become "all things large and small" emails. A course that had been intentionally conceived to unconventionally promote in-class interactive student and teacher "talk" about classic and contemporary literature through the lens of "waiting," now pivoted – a subject to change without notice! – into a course whose new foundation was to be the quantity and quality of each individual student's at-home analytical and creative writing. My active participants had effectively been silenced – shut up and shut down. Now it would be the voice of the class's writers that would be heard. Writing would henceforth be originating not in the college's calming but now abruptly closed library or during a subway ride to class from your full-time job but, instead, writing would be squeezed in and eek-ed out in a roommate's small and dark living room, or in a suddenly-shared bedroom-as-office, or on a makeshift desk smack against the kitchen stove, or on a married sister's small dinner table next to a rambunctious nephew who could not quite understand why, if you were "visiting," you had no time to play with him.

When I began this introduction to HEY, PROFESSOR, I said that as a teacher I "knew" or "sort of knew" my students from their classroom participation and from their written work. Yet now my course would be morphing from one in which I came to know them through their oral insights (from their seats, from within a collaborative group over in a corner of the classroom, from the front of the room with their backs to the chalkboard) to one in which I would primarily come to know them from how perceptively they individually wrote at home alone in response to my canned prompts for critical thinking.

Interestingly, I had had, only a week before distance learning was officially initiated, a very hide-in-plain-sight student tell me (privately, of course) that he would like my approval for his novel plan to avoid all student-to-student interaction in the course: he would substitute for engagement in any class "talk," handwritten examples of his own private thinking produced wherever he studied. Did this student somehow know that distance learning was on the horizon? Be careful what you tell your professor you wish for!

Yet, in theory, this audacious plan would also be a godsend to those students who just seemed never to be able to make it to class on time or hardly at all because of full-time work responsibilities, or family commitments, or personal lifestyles. When we did in fact go on to distance learning – when we went from an unclear absence policy to absence as policy – although my student-with-a plan flourished, my two principal classroom absentees never managed to find the sheltered-at-home time to do much of the written work of the course – neither the many creative pieces that had always been imagined at home to the newly increased number of more standard analytical pieces.

But the key change in the teaching and learning experience that I had after the tenth of March (the night we last met as a class act on campus) was that the medium of emails – of all things! – changed how I "sort of knew" my current students. I certainly sort of knew them differently, if not better. In my mind I came to think of our regular email correspondence as a kind of literature with its own narrative arc: my students' emails told the larger story of what it was like to be a hard-working, grade-conscious, stressed-out, worried, graduation-driven, career-ambitious college student in New York City – both B.C. and A.D. (Before Coronavirus, After Distancing).

As I daily read these sometimes pithy, sometimes prolonged emails – starting in the second week of March and mostly ending by the third week of May but also, in some cases, arriving well into June – I learned through their "Hey, Professor"-type salutations and their "take care" closings what it meant for them to go from being a highly motivated student on a diverse college campus to being a wounded, worried, and isolated human being trying (and sometimes failing) to "wait out" the practical, the physical, the mental and emotional and psychological personal emergencies that are inevitable when a worldwide health crisis hits home.

These back-and-forth emails are this book – portraits of pandemic pedagogy, if you will, or the aloneness of the long distance learner. Amazingly, working from our respective homes twenty-seven of my students and I wound up collaborating as writers of a book – a book about "waiting" but also a book about how we wound up together creating a course that my students had believed already existed in my head, a course they originally thought they would be *taking,* not *making.* (The book has been published as SOME DAY: THE LITERATURE OF WAITING – A CREATIVE WRITING COURSE WITH TIME ON ITS HANDS.)

But this is not that book. HEY, PROFESSOR is our *other* book – the one about remote teaching and learning on the college level, about the almost solitary study of serious literature, about the anxious (eager and nervous) lives of distant students. HEY, PROFESSOR is also, it turns out, a book about what it means to be young, urban, and ambitious; it's about how school work can keep you sane or make you think you're this close to going over the edge; it's about how the humanities don't lend themselves to the "keep-six-feet apart" rule and is not really a subject to change; it's about how one day can so blend into the next that you don't really know what day it is – and sometimes wonder whether that even matters (it does if you have to send the professor an email with a pdf attachment of your not-late writing).

But more than anything (from Christina's opening apology to Shanya's closing critique), HEY, PROFESSOR is a portrait gallery of personal stories about the need to keep calm and be kind, to stay well (or get better), to move on and work toward – as best you can. In effect, to use a phrase that comes up again and again in its emails, it is a book that tries to remind us that the most essential human thing is to "take care."

Paradoxically, Our On-Campus Special Topics Course on "The Literature of Waiting" Sort of Begins Online With Two Electronic Blackboard Announcements from the Instructor and a Couple of Early Email Responses from His Students

Welcome message from Professor Eidelberg (his first of what will be regular twice-a-week online Blackboard announcements for the 14-week duration of "The Literature of Waiting" course)

January 21, 2020 / Hello, Colleagues,

Hello, all 28 (and counting!) of you (from upper freshman to upper senior) who have registered as of today, Tuesday the 21st of January, for the brand-new English Department special topics course "The Literature of Waiting" (English 25146-01).

Also brand-new – and this is of "timely" importance – is that our class will now meet in Hunter West Room 404 – and NOT on the fifteenth floor of Hunter North with eight of its ten elevators not currently in service. Please do not go first to Hunter North Room 1516 to check out any written notice to confirm this room change because (1) Hunter may not get around to posting such a notice, and (2) it will take you at least a half hour (I know!) to walk from that empty classroom down the fifteen flights of stairs, and (3) this course is about "wait," not "weight."

It doesn't go without saying (so I'll say it) that I am truly looking forward to meeting you – or to use the first of what I'm afraid will be a plethora of plays on the word "wait": I can't wait to meet all of you (including – no, especially – at least three of you from my other special topics course, "The Teacher and Student in Literature," from the fall 2019 and fall 2018 semesters).

Please be on time or early (but no later than 5:35 pm) for our first class session on Tuesday, January 28, as I have a full 75-minute participatory session planned for us that will also include the distribution of the course of study and syllabus, a colleague profile, a Calendar of Sessions with assignments for the first quarter of the course, and a hefty (but free!) COURSEPACK containing short and excerpted works of fiction on time, endurance, hope and expectation. (ALL of the course's several required

5

longer works should be purchased together immediately; they are in stock at Shakespeare and Co. bookstore but, truth be told, not in sufficient quantity because of the late surge in registration for the course.)

Awaiting your arrival (my largest class ever in my years at Hunter),

Bob Eidelberg

Adjunct Lecturer, The Literature of Waiting

Hunter College English Department

And now, let's hear it from the course's first emailers

January 24, 2020 (four days before Day 1 of our "we-can't-wait-for-it" course),

Dear Professor Eidelberg,

I hope all is going well with you! I am the student that met with you last semester during spring registration time to introduce myself and to discuss my possible interest in taking your Hunter College class next semester on "The Literature of Waiting" because I love to participate in philosophical class discussions. I'm really excited, and I can tell you are, too! Looking forward to an amazing semester!

Henry

Flash forward, for just a moment, to March 12, 2020, and to Professor Robert Eidelberg's online Blackboard announcement of the end of the course's existence (and, presumably, its potentially "amazing" philosophical discussions)

"Regrettably, our Tuesday, March 10, class of "The Literature of Waiting" course will be our last one to be held on campus; we will shortly become part of a City University of New York experiment in something called distance learning (and teaching?). Wait for it!"

March 12, 2020 / a response from that same "excited" student who sent the January 24 email)

Dear Professor Eidelberg,

That was a painful-to-read Blackboard announcement! It's really unfortunate that we won't be having any more in-person classes.

Henry

But back to the start of it all in January, seven weeks before the new normal of pandemic-induced remote humanities instruction began

January 29 / Hello, Colleagues (some brand-new to arrive on Thursday),

I hope you feel the way I do that Tuesday's first session of "The Literature of Waiting" promises a term worth waiting for (are teaching and learning a kind of "waiting"?). Class participation (fully 55 percent of your course grade) was so extensive that I already know at least half of your names by heart (but don't change the area of the room you sat in quite yet, although you can sit anywhere you like starting next week). As to the 14 or so of you whose names I do not know as yet, you know what you need to do at least twice during Thursday's session for me to learn them this week.

Now for some changes and clarifications in the reading and writing due for tomorrow's class based on all that's mentioned in the Calendar of Sessions for Days 1 and 2:

o   as you read the text of WAITING IS NOT EASY! and take scribbled notes on the prompt question about a change in its title, please also take scribbled notes on the changing attitudes of the TWO "waiters" in the story as revealed by the illustrated changes in their facial expressions and body language from cartoon panel to cartoon panel (these various attitudes might, in fact, be some of the different ways that human beings wait for something they are told is a "surprise"). Of course, this kind of reading will also help you in deciding which words to steal from author/ illustrator Mo Willems' text in order to create a poem of your own (following the guidelines for the CW/HW (Creative Writing

Homework) assignment at the bottom of the Session #1 entry and then repeated in smaller almost unreadable type at the top of the Session #2 entry);

o   check to see that somewhere in your COURSEPACK folder you have Chapter 1 from the Henry James novel THE WINGS OF THE DOVE. This 700-page novel (not even an optional read for this course!) begins with, of all things, the two words "She waited ...." (If you want to get a head start on this, read the first five or so pages – up to where the father arrives in the scene – and begin a formal list of all the different specific ways in which the daughter's behavior is a kind of waiting.)

Collegially,

Bob Eidelberg

January 29 / Good Afternoon Professor Eidelberg (from Shanya, one of several students who had received an A+ from me last semester in "The Teacher and Student in Literature" course),

First I'd just like to say how awesome it was to be back in your classroom yesterday with my former (and current colleague) Patrick! It was something I truly waited for and heavily anticipated over winter break. I was able to go through my COURSEPACK and I realized that I am missing three items: "The Odyssey" excerpt, the "Waiting for Godot" commentary, and the excerpts from the book-length essay "Passing Time."

Collegially,

Shanya

January 29 / Hello, Shanya,

Awesome for me, too! Thanks for the thorough check on the COURSEPACK materials. It turns out your pack is perfect: the first two items wound up becoming part of the ON WAITING materials (and shouldn't have been listed separately) and the PASSING TIME excerpts are in the process of being translated from the original German (didn't expect that explanation, did you?) and will come to you as a separate handout.

Well done — and again thanks for the accounting.

Collegially,

Bob Eidelberg

Christina is a graduating senior who starts the course by being unavoidably absent for its opening session. Christina lives in the borough of Queens and commutes to Hunter College's Manhattan campus at East 68th Street and Lexington Avenue by subway. Christina is majoring in sociology and minoring in gender/women's studies; she is planning on a career in social work after going to graduate school in the fall and completing her Master's degree.

Initially relatively shy in class, Christina had become a fairly active participant in our collegial on-campus discussions by the time, seven weeks later (at almost the exact mid-point of the term), that our class on "The Literature of Waiting" was silenced by the coronavirus pandemic and thrown into (and by) distance learning. A solid "A" student on mid-course March 10, Christina opted, for mental health reasons, just days before the class's final "session" on May 7 to take an Incomplete final grade in order to complete the course on her own and to her own satisfaction by the first of July (which she did, for a well-earned "A").

Portrait of On-Campus Christina

January 28 / Hello Professor Eidelberg,

I hope this email finds you well. I am Christina and am enrolled in your Literature of Waiting course (T/TH 5:35 pm). I wanted to let you know that I am currently stuck out of state at a family gathering for the Lunar New Year and will not be able to attend the first class tonight. I wanted to check in with you about any important materials or information I may be missing in tonight's class. I saw in the Blackboard announcement that we will be having a 75-minute participatory session and that course packets/ readings will be distributed in class – do I need to make up any work for this session and will I be able to pick up the materials on Thursday in class?

I will be in class on the 30th (Thursday) and look forward to this semester in your course!

Thank you so much,

Christina

January 28 / Hello, Christina,

Nice to make your acquaintance but sorry to learn that it won't be in person tonight. I "await" your arrival on Thursday; it would be a good idea to meet with me early outside our classroom — Hunter West (404) — at around 5:15 pm (if that is at all possible) so that I can make time to give you all the several materials I'll be distributing tonight and so that you can fill out one of them and glance over the others before Thursday night's class begins.

One thing you can do before Thursday is to write and bring with you a short poem or paragraph (or draw a sketch) that could appear under the title of "WAITING."

Happy new year to you and your family!

Collegially,

Bob Eidelberg

January 28 / Hello Professor Eidelberg!

I am not able to arrive at 5:15, as I have a class before that ends at 5:25 pm and only leaves me a 10-minute span to arrive "early." Would this be enough time to receive the material? I'm sorry for the inconvenience. For the poem/paragraph/sketch, are there any other criteria? Or would the piece just have to be related to "waiting"? Is there anything else that I should be preparing for Thursday's class? Thank you for the new year wishes, and I look forward to meeting you in person on Thursday!

Best,

Christina

January 28 / Hello again, Christina,

Not incidentally: notice how TIME — a major concept in any course on WAITING — has already played a part in your involvement in our course and your inability to come to class early on Thursday! Not to worry NOW — we both will deal with it.

As to the WAITING piece of writing, no other criteria (except legibility!) — just somehow connected to WAITING. Everything else due on Thursday can only be done by you if you know someone in the class, can contact them by phone, and can get them to read aloud to you over the phone a short work of literature we experienced together in class and then tell you its follow-up homework assignment. If that's not possible, I'll catch you up SOON enough.

Collegially,

Bob Eidelberg

January 29 / Greetings—

I hope all is well today. I do not yet have the contact information of another student in the class and am unable to give them a call about the piece and assignment. Will this affect when I am in class tomorrow?

Best,

Christina

Christina's piece of free writing on "Waiting" submitted on Thursday, January 30, her first day attending class:

Sitting
Tapping my feet
> *Tap. Tap. Tap.*
Glancing up at the clock,
> *I sigh.*
Once.
Twice.
Over and over …
> *until this time is finally over.*

February 7 / Hello Professor Eidelberg,

I have put the lyrics to my chosen published song in this email. I apologize that I forgot to bring the hard copy to class last night.

Thank you,

Christina

Portrait of Distance-Learner Christina

March 10 / Good afternoon, Professor,

I hope this email finds you well. I wanted to send an email because I read through President Raab's email about Hunter College continuing activities as usual, and was wondering if any professors have decided to hold their lectures online at any point / have any alternatives to simply conducting activity as is?

I understand that there has been mass hysteria about the coronavirus, and a lot of fear is unfounded. Though, I am concerned about traveling through the crowded subway system (as I take three separate trains to get to school) and just to get to such an over-populated campus; but I have anxiety about possibly missing classes as well.

I plan on attending classes, but I wanted to reach out to see what my professors were thinking during this situation.

Best,

Christina

March 11 / Hello Professor Eidelberg,

CUNY (City University of New York) has put out a statement about classes going online for distance learning on their Twitter account and I attached the screenshots.

March 14 / Hello Professor Eidelberg,

Here are my responses for the prompts.

THE STORY OF JACOB AND RACHEL: I think that this Biblical story is included by men in this story because it depicts a "proper" (traditional) familial situation where a man does as he is supposed to, by fulfilling the requirements of the father of the bride, without complaint. It depicts the father taking "proper" measures to get his eldest daughter wed first, and this may reflect a superstition/rule/practice within the faith. The story illustrates the value of patiently waiting for a betrothed and working diligently for your to-be father-in-law, while illustrating the practice of men negotiating the marriages/lives of women (showing that the norm of this society is patriarchy). The ending where God gives Leah baby boys aids in the teachings of patriarchy (sons are coveted and women that can give their husbands sons are highly valued). I think that this patriarchal structure speaks to the Abrahamic religions' teachings as they traditionally value the patriarchal structure and valuing/attributing blessings to their God, as God gave Leah sons and made Rachel barren (with Leah not having any more children once she attributed the blessing to God instead of her husband). The story also shows that appearance should not be more valued than a woman who is faithful to the faith and to her husband, as depicted by the fates of Rachel and Leah.

March 21 / Hello Professor Eidelberg,

I hope this email finds you well. I am sorry about sending you my work for Thursday so late, but I have attached my responses to this email. I have been staying with my partner's family during this chaos and have been struggling with my mental and, subsequently, my physical health. I have not been able to quiet the anxiety that I have been feeling for a few days and it has been giving me frequent chest pains and headaches so I have been slow to get through the first few chapters of the novel and my assignments. I did not want to worsen my anxiety by being hard on myself for submitting this assignment late, but I compromised by deciding to catch up with my work by this weekend and only have one assignment that is submitted late. So I apologize that this assignment is late but I plan to get everything else in on time, moving forward. This virus/quarantine/pandemic situation has been very hard in every situation and I very much regret not trying to find a therapy center sooner, but I am trying my best, as everyone else is doing.

Best,

Christina

March 22 / Hello Professor Eidelberg,

I hope this email finds you well. I have attached my Kate Croy poem to this email.

March 23 / Hello Professor Eidelberg,

I have attached my letter to Penelope from a suitor.

Best,

Christina

March 23 / Hello, Christina,

Many thanks — but it seems I cannot copy your letter from Penelope's suitor onto the pages of our course's book SOME DAY (in Microsoft Word).

Would you be able to send his letter to me as a pdf or some other form that is not part of a new email?

Collegially,

Bob Eidelberg

P.S. This will also be necessary for any further requests from me for your terrific CW/HWs.

March 26 / Hello Professor Eidelberg,

I hope this email finds you well. I have attached my responses to the Session 17 prompts.

Thank you,

Christina

March 27 / Hello, Christina,

Glad to have heard from you and more than glad that you have begun to work through the pandemic anxieties that you are not alone in feeling; in fact, please read (or re-read) my latest Blackboard announcement in which I slow us all down on what might have been a too "fast and furious" pace established by me at the very start of our course's distance learning, forgive any late WAITING FOR THE BARBARIANS assignments to date, and postpone the reading, thinking, and writing of an entire session of our course from next Tuesday to next Thursday (we all get to take a collective breath).

So here's to putting the "well" back in "welcome back"!

Collegially,

Bob Eidelberg

March 31 / Hello Professor Eidelberg,

I hope this email finds you well. I have attached my responses to the novel and the poem for Session 18 to this email.

Thank you,

Christina

March 31 / Hello Professor Eidelberg,

I have attached my WAITING FOR LEFTY piece to this email as requested by your previous email.

Thank you,

Christina

Christina's piece – a 2020 Coronavirus Pandemic Version of the Intern Vignette from Clifford Odets' 1935 play WAITING FOR LEFTY – was selected for publication in the course's book SOME DAY: The Literature of Waiting / A Creative Writing Course With Time on Its Hands

March 31 / Hello Professor Eidelberg,

I hope this email finds you well. I have attached my Lin journal entry in connection with Ha Jin's novel WAITING.

Thank you,

Christina

March 31 / Hello, Christina,

Please check in by email with all the other members of your group (see below). Also, as a favor to two of your group members: please telephone the two students I have asterisked and tell them (either directly on the phone or through a message that you leave) that they absolutely need to contact me right away at our course email glamor62945@mypacks.net and let me know definitively whether they are going to be distance-learning sending me and their group their required written work – Sessions #14 through #28 — as I have been asked by Hunter to officially notify the college by next week at the latest of the names of all students who have not yet started participating in distance learning for English 25146. Many thanks.

Collegially,

Bob Eidelberg

In response to the early impact of the coronavirus pandemic on our now completely off-campus student body, certain members of the administration of Hunter College emailed a communication to their faculty with the advisement that they notify students of Hunter's online counseling services and encourage those we thought might be in need. I immediately forwarded that email to about a third of my class.

April 3 / Hello, Colleagues,

Don't be hesitant to contact them if you are in need (see "Counseling for Students" email below).

Collegially,

Bob Eidelberg

Begin forwarded message:

Subject: Counseling for students
Date: April 3, 2020 at 8:44:27 AM EDT

In response to the early impact of the coronavirus pandemic on the now off-campus student body of Hunter College, the administration of the college sent the following policy communication to Hunter faculty with the advisement that they notify students and encourage those who might benefit from Hunter's counseling services to contact the Hunter College Counseling and Wellness Service, which would be operating remotely for them for the duration of distance learning.

April 22 / Hello, Christina,

I hope all is well with you since I have not heard from you or gotten written assignments in a couple of weeks. Please get back to me, okay?

Collegially,

Bob Eidelberg

P.S. Also, did I get an essay from you on your reading of ROBINSON CRUSOE and misplace it or did it somehow get lost in spam or suspect mail since it's not like you to have not done it?

April 30 / Hello Professor Eidelberg,

I hope this email finds you well, healthy, and safe. I am sorry for the late reply, as I have been struggling with quarantine and all of the chaos in the world recently. I also apologize for my lack of turning in assignments—it has been a great source of anxiety and fear, in all honesty. I hate that I am so behind in my classes, and I feel guilty that I am, but my mental health has been making doing anything difficult. It has been very difficult to get myself out of bed. I feel like the days are passing too quickly (because I can't start my day until late afternoon or evening), and my motivation has very much dropping due to just feeling so overwhelmed by everything that is going on.

This is my last semester at Hunter as an undergraduate student, and I feel very discouraged by my unproductive behavior during this online transition. I actually need to get all A's this semester to keep my scholarship (I dropped by .02 from where I am supposed to be because I had to drop two classes two semesters ago, due to mental health struggles), and I just want to graduate. I just need to "get my act together" and do my work "like normal," but I just feel so ... I don't even know the word to describe it—burnt out. That's it. I feel so burnt out from trying to balance my depression and anxiety as well as years of pushing myself in academics without break, and adding this quarantine-pandemic chaos, I am not functioning at optimal productivity. I have even considered dropping out, even though I had plans to go on to Master's at Silberman's School of Social Work, even though this is my last semester... because I feel so hopeless in myself and overwhelmed by the anxiety around doing my work and my future.

I am staying this quarantine at my boyfriend's family's house in New Jersey, and it has been an adjustment to live my day to day life from living with my family in Queens. The social dynamics have also been difficult because I've been struggling with figuring out how to interact with my partner's 8-year-old child (when I've never had any experience with children because I am close in age to my brother and am on the younger end of my cousin's age spectrum), who has mild behavioral problems.

19

It's just difficult to get him to listen to things I have to say if I'm teaching ("lecturing") him about something. Also due to this pandemic chaos, I have to wait until the end of this week to get a new charger pack for my laptop because it is not classified as essential right now.

I know that this is a lot to just unload in my email but I felt that I wanted you to understand why I have not been able to get to my work as productively as I'd like to ideally. As well as confide in you about my current mental and physical health. I have been sluggish, tired, unmotivated, lethargic, and plain struggling to do many tasks beyond existing from moment to moment. I am trying to research more resources for therapy, as I have neglected this for a few months ....

I WILL try my utmost to get through the work, but I wanted to let you know that my primary concern as a human right now is my mental health, so I am a bit slow to get through the assignments. I have very much enjoyed your (on-campus) class so much, and am very disappointed in myself for not being able to even get myself together enough to do even things I enjoy.

I hope you are healthy and well, & wish safety and well-being to all your loved ones.

Best, during this grueling, political, social distancing, period of chaos ("Waiting for the End of COVID-19"),

Christina

P.S. No, I unfortunately did not send the essay. I have been trying to work my way through listening to the audio reading on YouTube and reading a copy of the story online. I am so sorry, I know it is unlike me, and I know that all of these assignments are late. Better to do the work late and submit it all, than none at all.

May 1 / Hello, Christina,

I am so glad to hear from you and appreciate your confiding and "unloading." Of course I am sorry for all that you are going through — and I would like to propose a way forward to the extremely conscientious Christina that I first met via email back in January because she was upstate at a family event and would be missing the first class of our course.

Since the quite strong 95 you earned from me at the very mid-point of the course on March 10 (the equivalent of a high "A" or "A+") is the grade I would like to enter for you sometime after our course ends on May 7, I would like to suggest (please don't drop out!) that you authorize me to enter an "Incomplete" final course grade in mid-May and that you slowly take all the time from now until June 1 to complete as many of the missing assignments (or some of the replacement assignments detailed in my recent Blackboard announcements) as you can manage without stressing yourself out any further in these far from ideal times.

As you correctly put it, your priority right now is your mental health and not only should that not be neglected but any plan like the one I'm proposing needs to further your overall health, not interfere with it. So, please let me know what you think of this plan forward or if you have any "tweaks" to it that you'd like to make.

Get well soon in the ways that are best for you.

Collegially,

Bob Eidelberg

May 3 / Hello, Colleagues Who Have Been Privately Bcc'd This Personal Email,

Please give the email below your close attention. Thank you.

Collegially,

Bob Eidelberg

Begin forwarded message:

Hello, Selected Colleagues,

I hope you are physically and psychologically well during these stressful times since March 10, but I have noticed that since the start of distance learning you have not been fully involved in the work of our course as detailed in the Calendar of Sessions that you have in your possession (for Sessions #14 through #18, in particular) as well as in the changes, additions, and subtractions to the required reading and writing listed under those sections as detailed in six Blackboard announcements posted by me on a regular basis.

Besides from the fact that all CUNY faculty are now being asked to report the names of such students to, in your cases, Hunter College, I would like to reach out to you once again before I do anything in an official capacity that might jeopardize your status at Hunter. (Not so incidentally, I have sent personal email requests to several of you for pdf attachments of your first-rate pieces of creative writing done while we all were meeting together as a class on campus and those emails were neither complied with nor acknowledged.)

Seriously, I do hope you are reasonably okay, but I would feel a lot better if I knew that directly from you.

I hope you will respond to this email within the next day or so.

Collegially,

Bob Eidelberg

May 3 / Hello, Colleagues,

It's been a little while since I have heard from you either by a response to an email of mine, a Blackboard request, or a significant number of homework assignments turned in (even late), and I am concerned about your physical and mental health and your anxiety status during these worrisome times.

Also, I don't know whether you are doing any of the currently required reading in our "Literature of Waiting" course and are planning to send in some of the assigned written work (and/or optional replacement work) to me by this Thursday, May 7th, when our course officially has its last "session," but I do know that I will have to enter a course letter grade for you in the following weeks.

Some of your colleagues in our class have already opted for an arrangement in which I enter a grade of "Incomplete" on May 11th and then, after sufficient quality work has been turned in by a given date (June 1st, for example), I officially change the "Incomplete" to a passing grade of at least B+ (but higher letter grades are still possible).

Others have told me that such an extension (even to July 1st) would not work for them in their current stressful situation and that they would prefer that I give them an actual final passing grade on May 11th (one based on the numerical grade earned at the mid-point in the course on March 12th, plus or minus the quantity and quality of the work done since we all started to shelter in place at home).

I would appreciate your giving your options in this difficult situation some thought and your getting back to me as soon as possible by return email with how you would like for both of us to proceed.

Many thanks – and please be well and stay as healthily productive as you can.

Collegially,

Bob Eidelberg

May 3 / Hello Professor Eidelberg,

I hope this email finds you well and in good health. May I opt for the second course of action for the end of the semester ("one based on the numerical grade earned at the mid-point in the course on March 12th, plus or minus the quantity and quality of the work done since we all started to shelter in place at home")?

It would greatly alleviate some anxiety and honestly, help me maintain a better mental mind frame while doing my work.

Best,

Christina

May 3 / Hello, Christina,

I think you have confused elements of both the first and second courses of action.

The "second course of action" is not the "Incomplete" to be changed in June but my entering on May 7 the grade earned for the entire term (probably lower than the mid-point grade), but not less than a "B."

The first course of action is the "Incomplete" on May 11 with a letter grade (probably an "A") to be entered by no later than July 1 (not the end of the summer — that's not possible).

It sounds to me like you actually want the first course of action, which gives you almost two months (the rest of May and all of June) to finish sending in your work (I would hope that you would not send it all on June 30 but, instead, send each assignment as soon as you complete it). Is this the plan you prefer?

Collegially,

Bob Eidelberg

May 3 / Hello—

Yes! I would like to take the incomplete, as it would give me more time to pace sending assignments to you.

Thank you,

Christina

May 11 / Hello, Professor Eidelberg,

I hope this email finds you well and healthy. I am sorry for the delay, but to give you an update on my state of mind—I feel a bit better!

I have attached my filled-out consent form for the SOME DAY book to this email. Please let me know if you can open the picture!

Thank you,

Christina

May 11 / Hello, Christina,

Yes, no problem opening the consent form email — and I'm so glad to hear that you are feeling a bit better. I'm confident you'll be able to build on that foundation.

All the best.

Collegially,

Bob Eidelberg

May 11 / Hello, Colleagues for whom I have already entered an "INC" (Incomplete) on the grade roster:

I am concerned that I have started to receive some missing and/or replacement work from ONLY 2 of the 9 of you that I have an agreement with, and I am already under some pressure to justify to Hunter College such a high number of INC grades in one course (fully a third of the class).

So, all nine of you, please start sending me work that I can point to as evidence that you are actually busy working right now to upheld your end of our agreement (regardless of the actual end date that we agreed upon a few weeks ago). I would hate to have the whole arrangement for all of you jeopardized by my inability to document that work is being sent to me by all of you on a fairly regular basis over the next weeks.

Thank you for your understanding.

Collegially,

Bob Eidelberg

May 19 / Hello Professor Eidelberg,

I hope this email finds you well and healthy. I have attached my essay for the incorporation or rejection of the novel ROBINSON CRUSOE as a work of literature to be used in the course next semester.

Best,

Christina

June 1 / Hello Professor Eidelberg,

I hope this email finds you well. I am sorry that I have not been able to get in all my assignments for today. I have not been feeling well and, honestly, my depression has been hitting me with an especially bad bout right now. I would really like to get through the entirety of the semester's work because I genuinely want to experience all of it. Would it be all right of me to ask if I could have until around the end of the week to submit the work for Sessions 22-28?

Also, I have to get the consent for your next book to you—and I will! I have been slowly getting back on my feet today and, honestly, my mental health seriously affects my physical health so I have been trying to cope with that too.

I was seriously thinking about writing a book about my college experience and my mental health – and I would love to know if you have any tips with writing books, the process, or anything you could enlighten me about because I think you are knowledgeable in this realm – and many others!

Best,

Christina

June 1 / Hello, Christina,

Please do not add to your stress by striving to complete the remaining assignments in such a short period of time. Our original agreement gave you until the end of June, not the end of May, so let's pace ourselves over the next 2-3 weeks, okay? And here's how because I so love your words about your desire to experience the whole course: just send me a piece of make-up work as you complete it and before you start in on the next. I'm in no hurry to change the Incomplete to an A within the next few days – the next few weeks works well for me if it works well (important word, that "well") for you.

As to your book idea, my new book "Hey, Professor" already has plans to use excerpts from your emails to me as one of the first portraits in the book on the nexus of mental health and college learning, but if you want to also pursue this in some personal writing on your own, I would encourage it as both excellent therapy for yourself and as potential instructive help for your readers. Whatever its final form, perhaps the initial form should be a journal of your daily thoughts, feelings, ideas, questions, etc. on the effect of your mental health on particular college experiences you are having this semester (and how distance learning has helped or hurt). Or, anecdotal-type short stories – each about one or another of such experiences from past semesters.

Get better, stay well (as well as you can without getting sick over the effort), keep in touch.

Collegially,

Bob Eidelberg

June 18 / Hello to the Four English 25146 "Incomplete" Colleagues Who Have Until June 30 to Submit Their Missing Homework Assignments and Replacement Work,

I hope you four are relatively well and working on your assignments relatively diligently.

As I've mentioned previously, on the first of July I must officially contact Hunter College and inform them of which letter grade your Incomplete is to be changed to. Since I have not received much work from some of you in recent weeks (despite my stressing the importance of your sending me each piece as you complete it so that I have time to read it carefully and evaluate it fairly), I am concerned that I will be inundated with lots of writing from the four of you in the last three days of June.

Here's how I feel about that: with so little time for me to read and evaluate that much work, it is highly unlikely that any of you would wind up with a mark of A- or A. If that is not an actual concern for you, I would have no problem entering a mark of either B or B+ (depending) for you on next Monday, June 22, based on my record of all that you have done and done well both in our thirteen on-campus classes and since distance learning began after March 10. If that works for you, please let me know right away.

And if you still want the time until June 30 to work at home some more to get a final course grade of A- or A, then you MUST send me something substantial that you have recently written for the course by that same date — next Monday, June 22.

If you have any questions about any of this, of course email them to me immediately.

Collegially,

Bob Eidelberg

July 1 / Hello, Christina,

Just wanted to let you know that based on your meeting our July 1 deadline with a sufficient number of quality pieces of written work (made-up missing assignments, replacement assignments, extra-credit pieces), I have formally requested Hunter College to change your Incomplete to a final letter grade of "A" in The Literature of Waiting course. (I don't know whether you completed all your reading of Beckett's WAITING FOR GODOT as that was the one work of lit for which I got only some of the written assignments; of course, knowing the kind of student you are, I recommend the play for some less-frenetic reading over the next couple of weeks.)

Most of all, though, congratulations on what was a far from easy or easily assumed academic achievement in these troubled times. Have a stress-free, healthy, and happy summer!

Collegially,

Bob Eidelberg

July 3 / Hello Professor Eidelberg,

I hope this email finds you well. I have seen my grade and would like to take the letter grade ("A") and not the CR (Credit) mark for the course.

Thank you for a wonderful semester. I am still working on Godot, nonetheless!

Best,

Christina

Valeria is a senior who is hoping to graduate at the end of the summer. Valeria came to the United States from Peru in 2002 and now lives as a recently married woman in Brooklyn, New York. Valeria is majoring in clinical psychology, works full-time as an operations specialist for Apple, and would like to become a clinical psychologist. Valeria is one of three students in "The Literature of Waiting" course who had me as their teacher (Valeria under her non-hyphenated maiden name) for my other special topics English Department course on "The Teacher and Student in Literature."

Valeria began "The Literature of Waiting" course pretty much the same way she had begun "The Teacher and Student in Literature": always attentive to the ideas of her colleagues in the class but generally reluctant to share hers aloud with them and with the instructor. Her progress in participation was gaining steam just as distance learning went into effect early in March and took the wind out of her. Distance learning further complicated Valeria's already fairly overwhelming life in which she struggles to balance work, family, and school; she was one of four students still working well into June when she decided to accept a less stressful final grade of B+ for all she had accomplished to date.

Portrait of On-Campus Valeria

January 30 / Hello Professor Eidelberg,

I apologize, but unfortunately have to miss class today. My mother had a medical emergency yesterday morning and just came home from the hospital. I will be staying with her to make sure she's taken care of. I apologize again for missing class and if you need any documentation to verify my absence please let me know. I have a classmate's contact information and will reach out to them about anything important I have missed.

Thank you,

Valeria

February 11 / Hello Professor Eidelberg,

I hope you had a good weekend. I wanted to reach out and raise a concern I was having. I have heard you mention to some students a few times that all of the required books for the course must be bought in the printed format. I do have some of the books (3 of them) in print, because that was the most cost efficient for those specific books, but I also did purchase some in e-book format, because it was more cost efficient. I completed all of my book purchases before the semester even began in mid-January and before I knew that you would not allow e-book format and at this point I cannot return them. I am not sure where to go from here as I cannot afford to purchase them once again in print.

Valeria

February 11 / Hello, Valeria,

Let's talk specifics before class tonight, okay? Which books, by the way, did you buy in paperback format (new or used)?

Collegially,

Bob Eidelberg

February 11 / Hello, Professor Eidelberg,

Thank you for getting back to me. I have 3 of the required books, The Haunting of Hill House, The Dumb Waiter, and The Caretaker, and I am still waiting to receive the three plays by Odets in the mail. I will see you before class.

Thank you,

Valeria

Portrait of Distance-Learner Valeria

March 19 / Hello Professor,

I've been going over your Blackboard announcements and emails but I cannot find specific instructions to where you will be hosting lectures. I looked under Blackboard collaborate ultra and cunywebex. Are lectures going to be held in real time? Or will it just be us emailing you our responses to the readings and prompts.

Thank you,

Valeria

March 20 / Hello Professor Eidelberg,

Attached is the first assignment due as part of our new curriculum.

I am enjoying the novel "Waiting for the Barbarians." It is interesting especially as someone who feels a sort of kinship with the barbarians, since I am an immigrant myself. I feel like I can read further than what the narrator is giving us. I will admit that there are parts in the novel that I don't understand but it is interesting either way.

Best,

Valeria

April 20 / Hello Professor Eidelberg,

I hope everything is well and you are staying safe during this difficult time. I have been meaning to reach out but I have been occupied with a lot of things since the city was shutdown. I have been feeling very overwhelmed as I have had to take on many new responsibilities since my family has been affected in so many ways by the virus. My husband works in a hospital as a nurse attendant and still has to go into work, which means that I have to handle things in my house as well as my parents' house, who have both lost their jobs and are too scared to leave their house due to the current health crisis.

Having to juggle feeding and taking care of everyone while now having to work from home has left me not being able to balance work, family, and school. I apologize for not reaching out sooner. At first I felt like I could get a handle on everything and then I had fallen so far behind that I was struggling to keep up. I really would like to be able to finish out the semester since I am only a few credits away from graduating, but I am not sure where to start, and I would really hate to withdraw from any of my classes. I am not sure if you would be willing to help me get back on track with the course work but would appreciate it greatly.

Best,

Valeria

April 22 / Hello Professor Eidelberg,

I am attaching my work for Session 23 on "Merrily We Roll Along." As I was completing the reading of the way the musical was written I was reminded of one of my favorite musicals that plays with time as well, "The Last Five Years." It's about two individuals whose story begins at the end of their relationship for one character and for the other at the beginning. In the end, the character who began singing at the end finds themselves at the beginning of the story and the other character at the end of the story – both characters' timelines meet at the middle of the musical with a song called "The Next Ten Minutes," which uses that phrase to allude to this idea of forever.

Best,

Valeria

May 3 / Hello, Colleagues Who Have Been Privately Bcc'd This Personal Email,

Please give the email below your close attention. Thank you.

Collegially,

Bob Eidelberg

Begin forwarded message:

Hello,

It's been a little while since I have heard from you either by a response to an email of mine, a Blackboard request, or a significant number of homework assignments turned in (even late), and I am concerned about your physical and mental health and your anxiety status during these worrisome times.

Also, I don't know whether you are doing any of the currently required reading in our "Literature of Waiting" course and are planning to send in some of the assigned written work (and/or optional replacement work) to me by this Thursday, May 7th, when our course officially has its last "session," but I do know that I will have to enter a course letter grade for you in the following weeks.

Some of your colleagues in our class have already opted for an arrangement in which I enter a grade of "Incomplete" on May 11th and then, after sufficient quality work has been turned in by a given date (June 1st, for example), I officially change the "Incomplete" to a passing grade of at least B+ (but higher letter grades are still possible).

Others have told me that such an extension (even to July 1st) would not work for them in their current stressful situation and that they would prefer that I give them an actual final passing grade on May 11th (one based on the numerical grade earned at the mid-point in the course on March 12th, plus or minus the quantity and quality of the work done since we all started to shelter in place at home.

I would appreciate your giving your options in this difficult situation some thought and your getting back to me as soon as possible by return email with how you would like for both of us to proceed.

Many thanks – and please be well and stay as healthily productive as you can.

Collegially,

Bob Eidelberg

May 5 / Hello Professor Eidelberg,

I hope you are continuing to stay safe and healthy. Thank you for reaching out. I know we emailed a little bit ago about the coursework and how I could proceed. I was able to complete the work for Session 23 and sent that to you. Recently the company that I work for has increased the workload they are requiring for me to complete at home in order for them to continue to pay me, which has made it difficult for me to catch up and keep up with everything else at the same time. I read over you recent email and think that perhaps completing the coursework by a later date by receiving the grade of incomplete would be the best option for me. This semester has been rough, before everything occurred I registered for more classes than I usually do in order to graduate this summer, something I would not have done had I known what everything would be like now. I think completing everything by a future deadline would be best since I am only taking one other class this summer and it will help me balance with everything that is going on. Again thank you for your understanding and cooperation.

Valeria

June 5 / Hello Professor Eidelberg,

I hope you are well and staying safe and close to your loved ones amid these increasingly difficult times. I am attaching a pdf of the work originally assigned for Session 17 on "Waiting for the Barbarians," which I had started reading back toward the end of March and was finding interesting and enjoying, as I wrote you.

Thank you,

Valeria

June 18 / Hello to the Four English 25146 "Incomplete" Colleagues Who Have Until June 30 to Submit Their Missing Homework Assignments and Replacement Work,

I hope you four are relatively well and working on your assignments relatively diligently.

As I've mentioned previously, on the first of July I must officially contact Hunter College and inform them of which letter grade your Incomplete is to be changed to. Since I have not received much work from some of you in recent weeks (despite my stressing the importance of your sending me each piece as you complete it so that I have time to read it carefully and evaluate it fairly), I am concerned that I will be inundated with lots of writing from the four of you in the last three days of June.

Here's how I feel about that: with so little time for me to read and evaluate that much work, it is highly unlikely that any of you would wind up with a mark of A- or A. If that is not an actual concern for you, I would have no problem entering a mark of either B or B+ (depending) for you on next Monday, June 22, based on my record of all that you have done and done well both in our thirteen on-campus classes and since distance learning began after March 10. If that works for you, please let me know right away.

And if you still want the time until June 30 to work at home some more to get a final course grade of A- or A, then you MUST send me something substantial that you have recemntly written for the course by that same date — next Monday, June 22.

If you have any questions about any of this, of course email them to me immediately.

Collegially,

Bob Eidelberg

Nathalie (with an "h," although she was somewhat blasé about its necessity when I asked early on in the term) was born in France and came to the United States in 2004. Nathalie lives in Manhattan while attending Hunter College, where she is a graduating senior majoring in political science. Nathalie's on-campus and at-home course comments about society, government, politics, educational philosophy and practice, you-name-it convinced her colleagues in "The Literature of Waiting" class that she had chosen the right major.

Nathalie really enjoys a good argument (and is really good at arguing); her spontaneous stimulation of the hearts and minds of her colleagues in class during our first seven weeks together on campus totally disappeared when we all became remote from one another. Nathalie plans to go to into the practice of law (if they'll have her, she says).

Portrait of On-Campus Nathalie

February 6 / Hello Professor,

I hope this reaches you well if at all – I am not so sure that this is the correct email through which to reach you but it is the one from which I received your welcome email back in late January.

After Tuesday's class, I thought again about your brief comment in response to my explaining some ideas of my found poem as mentioned in class. You had asked me, to my delight, if I was a philosophy major. While initially greatly complimented by your inquiry, I found it somewhat problematic upon further reflection.

You see, what I take issue with is the idea that certain ways of thinking, specifically, inquiries into the existential "problems," are to be cast off to one specific discipline. Furthermore, while this was not mentioned in our classroom, the discipline of philosophy carries many connotations, most notably that of being "for academics," "by academics," "impractical," and "unprofitable." As a whole, the sentiment you offered in good faith, the same one I took very kindly to, I think represents a deeply seeded social ill that seeks to convince people, as a whole, that this kind of inquiry is not a priority.

While I do believe, and know, that this sentiment animates capitalist societies, and more specifically by those who intentionally try to preserve the shallow value systems which perpetuate such societies, I think our general inclination to box the "existential inquiry" into a category, such as philosophy, speaks more to the general horror that is really grappling with it.

Forgive me if this seems like an unfinished thought because it mostly is ... but I had an itch to share it nonetheless, as I think it is thematically inseparable from the topic of our class, Waiting.

Looking forward to class this evening!

Best,

Nathalie

February 9 / Hello, Nathalie (with the silent "h" and an itch to scratch),

You've certainly given me much to think about at home after I, apparently, gave you much to think about in class. I'm glad my asking you whether you were a philosophy major initially delighted you as it was, as I can see in your email that you understood, meant as a compliment. It's probably the highest compliment I, as both a teacher and a human being, give students (human beings who are more likely to "profitably" use their minds than other human beings I regularly come into contact with in my work, like some teachers at Hunter I sometimes encounter!).

Incidentally, my second highest compliment to a student would be to ask if she was "an English major studying literature" since that field is, in my opinion, quite philosophical — and foundationally practical if one wants to be a fully "human" being. Interestingly, my only true faculty colleagues at Hunter are members of either the Philosophy Department or the English Department and my "thematically inseparable" course on THE LITERATURE OF WAITING was promoted by handbills and "oral faculty and student testimonies" ONLY in those two departments (not even in Political Science!). Also, to the best of my memory, I have never asked a student of mine whether she was a computer science major (maybe because I could always tell!).

So, if you see where I'm going with this also "unfinished thought," let me say at this point that everything you say about my comment's being "problematic" was, coincidentally, the subject of an extended discussion I had back in December with certain Hunter colleagues who asked me about the kind of student I was seeking to attract to the WAITING AS EXISTENTIALISM course. Are you sure you were not within hearing distance of us, taking it all in? We could talk more about this if you'd like (before class since I generally arrive at 5:15) since not only does the discipline of philosophy get wrongly pigeonholed as purely "academic" so, increasingly, does the discipline of teaching literature.

Whereas he says in ending but not concluding (do I sound like a lawyer arguing a case that shouldn't need to be made?), every discipline in search of disciples needs to be conceived and taught under the rubric of "the philosophy of sociology, the philosophy of religion, the philosophy of history, the philosophy of mathematics...."

Scratching back your itch (with thanks),

Bob Eidelberg

February 10 / Hi Professor,

Thank you so much for your thoughtful response to my all-over-the-place "one more thing."

I realize now that my "itch" to follow up with you on this particular train of thought comes from the fact that I have only recently concerned myself with the exclusive rigor of many disciplines (and how I see it has come to organize our social values in a way that has serious implications) and understood (a notion which you have since confirmed in your above email!) from the first few classes of The Literature of Waiting that you are inclined to think the same way.

I do find it tough to parse out these particular, unfinished and unfinishing, thoughts in an email, and so will gladly take you up on your offer to chat more before class!

Another thanks and kind regards,

Nathalie

February 20 / Hello Professor,

I regrettably will not be able to make this evening's class as I am feeling progressively unwell since yesterday evening. My apologies, I do look forward to our bi-weekly discussions.

I'll be sure to reach out to some of my classmates to get notes on what I missed today.

Best,

Nathalie

February 27 / Hello Professor,

I just got notified that I need to cover a co-worker at an event tonight that begins at 6:00 PM downtown on 18th street. Due to this semi-urgent circumstance, I will unfortunately not be able to stay for class today but will be sure to stop by beforehand to hand in today's assignment.

Apologies!

Nathalie

March 5 / Hello Professor,

As this novel virus continues to spread, I am finding myself quite anxious over the idea that we are waiting for the government to get their act together to prevent the spreading of such illnesses when science and pathogen studies, including US Preparedness Reports, outline specifically that the country and international political economy are unprepared to actually deal with a situation like this, which is inevitably escalating.

Considering that less than 100 tests had been conducted in NYC up until yesterday, and the reports that two people who died two weeks ago in Washington had the illness, it is undoubtedly prevalent in our city of 8 million people. The fact that we have to wait for someone to decide it is worth it to test students before taking the necessary precautions is not only silly but dangerous.

I strongly believe that CUNY is on its way to being shut down temporarily in efforts to combat this virus, along with other city schools, but that it is a matter of when the government thinks it will be worth it to interfere. I find that showing up to school in the meantime simply because we have blind faith in an authority that has admitted they are in uncharted territory is dangerous to both students and the health of our overall global community.

I realize this may sound a bit ridiculous ... but I would rather edge on this kind of ridiculousness than the kind that sees what is going on in Seattle, Italy, etc., right now and not acting vigilantly enough, and without enough resources, to ensure the public in efforts to protect private interests.

Further, with a light unceasing cough, I was wondering if my taking absence from today's class would be penalized under these circumstances.

While I know that the nature of our class is participation-based and that that is difficult to supplement, I would truly appreciate knowing if there is a way that I can seriously address this personal concern of mine without jeopardizing my grades.

Best,

Nathalie

March 7 / Hello, Nathalie,

You've given me a lot to think about but for now my main concern is the current state of your health. Are you still coughing? Have you taken your temperature on a regular basis and have you been running a fever? What is it now and is that lower or higher than previously? Do you have health care of any kind and have you consulted a doctor or other medical practitioner?

Clearly you need to stay home if you are not truly well, no matter what the reason or cause — and, of course, do all that you can as a student in our course based on the Calendar of Sessions that you have, my on-going Blackboard announcements, and your telephone or email contacts with colleagues in our class. Let's not add worry about your ultimate course grade to your current medical concerns.

And please keep in touch. Naturally, I wish you the best in every respect.

Collegially,

Bob Eidelberg

March 10 / Hello Professor,

Thank you for your considerate response and kind wishes. As of Sunday night, I have started to feel a bit better – I was mostly just anxious over my current status of being uninsured, combined with the general lack of transparency in the handling of this situation.

Additionally, I see this correspondence as keeping in theme with the course ... waiting to recover ... waiting for what feels like a tipping point ... waiting for decisions to be made on the basis of something that is new and unknown ... waiting to know how long we will be waiting for....

While waiting, and our existential relationship to it, is often on my mind, the above state of waiting has been causing me more discomfort and disturbance than usual .... I wonder if it is because of a tendency to catastrophize, or because, due to the scale of those affected by this virus, the existential malaise feels that much greater.

Still having some sniffles, but seeing as CUNY has yet to suggest an alternative for in-person meetings (despite private NYC universities doing so and the Mayor suggesting that we avoid public transportation if possible ... sigh), I will see you later today!

Best,

Nathalie

Portrait of Distance-Learner Nathalie

March 11 / Hi Professor,

I wanted to follow up on our correspondence after the comments from yesterday's class.

I appreciate that you appreciated my relating my concerns to our course theme but did want to clarify a couple of the points you made yesterday.

In my initial email, I meant to convey that my anxiety is principally over the general mishandling of a novel disease. I did not mean to suggest that I was planning on taking absence for the rest of the semester over a cough and some congestion. I was more trying to use those symptoms to suggest that, yes, while the people my age are not at risk of severe illness or worse, we are all currently perpetuating the spread of something that people are refusing to take seriously simply because of that fact.

Additionally, your comments in regards to the consideration of endowments in regards to shutting campuses reaffirm my belief that those making decisions are putting the health of CUNY students, many of which are responsible for caring for their family members, including older family members of marginalized communities, below their interests. The fact that we don't have money to hold over any body's head does not make me think that Columbia faculty is overreacting but rather that Hunter and CUNY are underreacting because they don't face the same threats.

My "existential" anxiety is not that this disease will spread and kill the world, no, but rather that decisions are being made by those who are not experts in the field, and that all of this time in between trying to debate facts which are unclear and evolving is indicative of how little our well-being matters to the top dogs.

Having been intensely studying human responses to global catastrophes, it was clear to me since January that this would spread should there not be any mitigation. I believe that the lack of mitigation that has since allowed it to spread is a result of discourse which tells us to accept what we are hearing from authorities.

The tipping point I am waiting for is not for my health, but for the state of affairs. For two weeks it is clear that this was going to be declared a

43

pandemic, and waiting for those two weeks while acting like it isn't real until WHO says it is not only has made the problem worse but is generally leaving me at a loss in how to navigate a world which does not seem to be able to respond to facts that are uncomfortable because they challenge the values we base our day-to-day on.

More on this incomplete thought later ... thank you for taking the time to read and address my previous emails in class.

Best,

Nathalie

March 12 / Hi Professor,

Could you please let me know which group I am in for our independent book project? I must have missed it on the day of my absence last week.

Best,

Nathalie

March 12 / Hello, Nathalie,

It's the play ROSENCRANTZ AND GUILDENSTERN ARE DEAD by Tom Stoppard. You have the writing assignment that's due on March 31, right? And, not so incidentally, how are you?

Collegially,

Bob Eidelberg

March 12 / Hi Professor,

Thank you, Professor, for letting me know about which group is mine!

And yes, I do have the assignment.

Honestly, I am upset and relieved at the same time. It is so disappointing that the government waited until a situation that was clearly escalating so bad to act, that now millions of people's educations and lives are being disrupted for such a long period of time. It seems to me that, had precautions been taken earlier on in the course of this week's pathogen's spread, the height of it may have even been over by now, without such extreme measures having to be taken.

It's weird to me how we all tend to start taking things seriously when they affect us personally. I am relieved that things are now being taken seriously such that we can start moving towards overcoming this odd time of our lives, but utterly heartbroken that the measures now mean that I and others will not be able to finish off the semester on campus.

I'm sure my previous emails suggested an eagerness to not attend class; however, I think I was taking out my frustration that precaution, while often considered over-reactionary, works to avoid larger disruptions such as what we're seeing all over the globe and now experiencing in our own class. This whole mess is just frustrating, a bit scary and sad – I apologize for having berated you with my ongoing comments into it.

I hope the transition to online teaching goes smoothly and look forward to resuming lessons this week, despite not attending the class.

Best regards and good health,

Nathalie

March 18 / Hello, Colleagues,

A brief but really important message: if you currently do not have the email address of each and every other member of your independent reading group, please email me right away to get those email addresses you are missing.

In the next three weeks, not only will everyone in a group (and that's everyone!) be in direct contact with all their other group members as part of a soon-to-be-announced newly devised way for "oral communication" to again be a part of your independent reading assignment but also at least one other activity in our coursework before the end of the semester will require all group members to be in regular email contact and, perhaps, telephone/cellphone contact, with one another.

Start to think of your 5-person group as a mini-off-campus class in THE LITERATURE OF WAITING – one that I will also be involved in. Details to follow on the next several Blackboard announcements, so don't delay getting from me any contact information you are missing.

Collegially,

Bob Eidelberg

March 18 / Hi Professor,

Could you please send the emails of my group members?

Best,

Nathalie

March 19 / Hello Professor,

I wanted to let you know that I will likely be submitting today's assignment a bit late (by tomorrow), due to ongoing ramifications from the mitigation of this virus. Since the class was disrupted last week, I and several members of my family are now facing unemployment and I have thus been focusing my energy on trying to alleviate the consequences of these events.

I hope that this will be the last time such an inconvenience occurs in the course of our new online class.

Hope you and yours are in good health, both physically and emotionally.

Best,

Nathalie

March 25 / Hello Selected Colleagues,

I hope you are physically and psychologically well during these stressful times since March 10, but I have noticed that since the start of distance learning you have not been fully involved in the work of our course as detailed in the Calendar of Sessions that you have in your possession (for Sessions #14 through #18, in particular) as well as in the changes, additions, and subtractions to the required reading and writing listed under those sections as detailed in six Blackboard announcements posted by me on a regular basis.

Besides from the fact that all CUINY faculty are now being asked to report the names of such students to, in your cases, Hunter College, I would like to reach out to you once again before I do anything in an official capacity that might jeopardize your status at Hunter. (Not so incidentally, I have sent personal email requests to several of you for pdf attachments of your first-rate pieces of creative writing done while we all were meeting together as a class on campus and those emails were neither complied with nor acknowledged.)

Seriously, I do hope you are reasonably okay, but I would feel a lot better if I knew that directly from you.

I hope you will respond to this email within the next day or so.

Collegially,

Bob Eidelberg

P.S. Below, for your reference, is a sample of how you will need to send me all past-requested and in-the-future required pieces of creative writing in our course.

March 25 / Hi Professor,

Thank you for reaching out in regards to my lack of recent involvement in the class – I want to emphasize that this is not meant in any disrespect, but rather coming from my hard time coping with such dramatic shifts. I have been using the time to try and sort out these other material affairs .... I am hoping to be back on my academic track by this weekend once I help my father finalize a few of his affairs on how to best move forward given our familial circumstances.

Further, I will send you the assignments by tomorrow!

I hope you are well, healthy, and in good spirits.

Best,

Nathalie

March 30 / Hi Professor,

Attached are the pieces you requested! Let me know if there is anything outstanding you would like me to send over.

Best,

Nathalie

March 30 / Hello, Selected Colleagues,

I hope you and your loved ones are doing well; I have a favor to ask of you in these chaotic times. I would like to include in our course's book the first-rate work you did (a 95 or higher mark) on the several creative writing pieces you wrote earlier in the semester and up to the end of our on-campus class.

So, if you can, please send me within the next few days a pdf of any of those pieces that you would like to be considered for publication, such as the Kate Croy found poem, the letter to a friend inspired by a song, the coda to THE DUMB WAITER, the changes you made in the vignettes to WAITING FOR LEFTY, the creative writing you did in connection with WAITING, and especially, your "How to Be a Waiter" piece.

Many thanks. Stay well and calm, sane and productive, caring and kind to others.

Collegially,

Bob Eidelberg

April 4 / Hello Professor,

I wanted to follow up with you after our last correspondence. Since last week, things have unfortunately taken a turn for the worse, with two family members in the hospital and increasing financial tensions, such that I was not able to tackle the work I was already behind on. In addition to simply updating you, I was wondering if you could let me know which assignments I should divert my priorities to in the case I may not be able to get all of this done. I will do my best to get reorganized, it's just daunting with so much piled up.

I really regret the way that this has all unfolded, as I looked forward to thinking about and completing assignments from your class all semester, it just seems I can no longer quite think straight.

I hope you are staying healthy and sane,

Nathalie

April 13 / Hello Professor,

I just wanted to reach out and let you know that I am really appreciative of your willingness to accept late work. Just because I have not yet gotten to it does not mean that I do not intend on completing the assignments and sending them over whenever they are finished.

I hope you and yours are well,

Nathalie

April 21 / Hello Professor,

Attached is my piece on why I think my group's play, "Rosencrantz and Guildenstern Are Dead," is fit to replace the novel "Waiting" in future class curriculums. I am working on completing the rest of my outstanding assignments in a timely manner. Thank you again for your understanding and I would like to nevertheless apologize for the inconvenience.

Best,

Nathalie

April 21 / Hello, Nathalie,

Welcome back! First-rate piece on "R & G Are Dead" — so good that I'd like to publish it in our course's book SOME DAY. To do that, I need for you to re-send it on a pdf that I would then open.

Many thanks.

Collegially,

Bob Eidelberg

April 21 / Hello Professor,

Thank you for your kind comments! Attached is a slightly revised version of the pdf.

Hope you and yours are well.

Nathalie

April 23 / Hey, group members!

Attached is my poem.

Hope everybody is doing alright!

Nathalie

May 3 / Hello, Colleagues Who Have Been Privately Bcc'd This Personal Email,

It's been a while since I have heard from you either by a response to an email of mine, a Blackboard request, or a significant number of homework assignments turned in (even late), and I am concerned about your physical and mental health and your anxiety status during these worrisome times.

Also, I don't know whether you are doing any of the currently required reading in our "Literature of Waiting" course and are planning to send in some of the assigned written work (and/or optional replacement work) to me by this Thursday, May 7th, when our course officially has its last "session," but I do know that I will have to enter a course letter grade for you in the following weeks.

Some of your colleagues in our class have already opted for an arrangement in which I enter a grade of "Incomplete" on May 11th and then, after sufficient quality work has been turned in by a given date (June 1st, for example), I officially change the "Incomplete" to a passing grade of at least B+ (but higher letter grades are still possible).

Others have told me that such an extension (even to July 1st) would not work for them in their current stressful situation and that they would prefer that I give them an actual final passing grade on May 11th (one based on the numerical grade earned at the mid-point in the course on March 12th, plus or minus the quantity and quality of the work done since we all started to shelter in place at home.

I would appreciate your giving your options in this difficult situation some thought and your getting back to me as soon as possible by return email with how you would like for both of us to proceed.

Many thanks – and please be well and stay as healthily productive as you can.

Collegially,

Bob Eidelberg

May 4 / Hi Professor,

Thank you kindly for reaching out with the above options. As my performance indicates, my academics have been suffering in these times as I am still processing the loss of now two people who were dear to me and battling a daunting outlook on the future.

I am mostly concerned with passing my courses this semester so that I have a chance of keeping my law school scholarship. If possible, I would like to opt for a passing grade on May 11 denoted from my mid-point grade (of 94) and quality of work since. I will try to turn in more assignments by the final deadline as well. **(Note from Mr. Eidelberg: Nathalie was happy with the B+ earned on May 11.)**

Further, I was wondering if a scanned copy of the signed release for the book would work instead of mailing it?

Best,

Nathalie

May 5 / Hi Professor,

Attached below is the scanned copy of the signed release – let me know if you might need a clearer picture.

Nathalie

Nattapat (greater stress on the first syllable) is an upper freshman planning to major in the biological sciences towards a career in some area of environmental science. Nattapat came to the United States from Thailand in 2009 and commutes by subway to Hunter College in Manhattan from the Bronx. Although he missed the first day of our class (providing, as is his nature, a formal note for his excused absence), Nattapat had perfect attendance after that and, in fact, was so consistently early to class that I soon found myself regularly chatting with him and a few other early arrivals in the hallway outside our classroom's door as we all, in keeping with the course's theme, patiently and productively waited for the room to empty of another teacher's students.

Nattapat also soon became the student I could count on to personally hand out to other students as they entered the room motivating printed materials I had prepared for them to read while they waited for our starting time of 5:35 pm to roll around (and, often, as they finished the "dinner" they had started to eat on their subway ride to Hunter).

After a somewhat "wait-and-see" beginning as an active participant (he is one of the youngest students in the class), Nattapat became one of the course's colleagues most engaged in our class's discussions (as well as one of the writers of the highest number of "one more thing" emails to the instructor, all of them demonstrating a mature wisdom and wit). Just a couple of sessions before he and his colleagues got exiled into distance learning, I overhead another major participant tell Nattapat that he was THE student in the class that she always made certain to pay close attention to. (Note: Nattapat was, on May 11, one of just a handful of the course's credit-bearing students to receive the famous Eidelberg A+ as his final course grade.)

Portrait of On-Campus Nattapat

February 11 / Hello Professor Eidelberg,

One last thought: as we were discussing "waiting" in religion centering around the Judeo-Christian belief, I couldn't help but wonder about other religions. Not being very knowledgeable in most religions, my mind wonders to Buddhism. I feel that path to enlightenment is just a really long

53

"wait" to understand the universe. You spend years and years pondering human nature and desire, and that to me is just like a long wait to finally be able to understand and let go of worldly desires. In addition to that, the whole business about reincarnation can be seen as some really long waiting until you reach enlightenment and stop the cycle of rebirth. I bet those who became trees spent more time waiting than anyone of us, more time thinking too; maybe that's where most people have their last cycle.

Another thought, in the story "Journey to the West," there is a big theme about waiting as a form of repentance, I feel. Son Wukong (the monkey king) had to wait underneath the mountain until the priest came and released him to go on this long journey to reach India. Pigsy on the other hand had to join the long journey in order to be forgiven for his crime of bothering some of the holy maidens, and Sandy, well I can't remember what Sandy did, but he also had to join the journey as well. In the end I feel that the journey is one big metaphor for both the spiritual path to reach enlightenment being perilous and long, and also the long wait that one must go through in order to reach it. After all, you can't just force enlightenment onto yourself, you have to wait for life's experiences to help you reach it – but that's just my own idea about it.

February 12 / Hello, Nattapat,

Thank you for your "couldn't help but wonder" ONE MORE THING (or ONE LAST THOUGHT as you have renamed it). I love any time our in-class talks lead students to "wonder" and I would very much like you to briefly share these thoughts at the start of Thursday's class (okay?) from your own reading on enlightenment as "a really long wait to understand the universe."

Collegially,

Bob Eidelberg

February 12 / From Nattapat,

Okay, I don't mind briefly sharing my thoughts.

February 27 / Hello Professor Eidelberg,

I believe that Lin is just like a child. He never really had to wait for anyone before and so no opportunity to grow as a person. The kinds of thought he had at the ending of the book are thoughts that those who have experienced life at least for a little bit goes through. Like a child he hastily threw Shuyu away just because she doesn't look beautiful, he quickly jumped on board with Manna, not because of love but because she initiated and showed him attention. Lin distracted himself from growing up by simply letting life take its own path, the only real decision he made being to go to Muijia rather than stayed in the countryside and that was because of a teacher. Lin has never had to think for himself before and now he is given the opportunity to do so, leading to the identity crisis we see. In this sense, I thought that the story was somewhat "tough-minded."

Portrait of Distance-Learner Nattapat

March 11 / Hello Professor Eidelberg,

It has come to my attention that CUNY colleges will be closed starting tomorrow until the 18th and then there will only be online classes until the end of the semester, a news I'm sure many have waited for – and dreaded. My question is: what will be the plan of operation for the up-coming classes? Will we be sending in our assignments online?

Waiting patiently, yet filled with confusion,

Nattapat

March 12 / Hello Professor Eidelberg,

Here are some of the assignments that are due. I believe I turned in my personal waiting journal-inspired piece, the question about "A Telephone Call," the revised vignette from "Waiting for Lefty" and an extra-credit assignment in hard copy. Please tell me if you have not received the physical copies. Here are my thoughts on some of the readings.

Nattapat

March 14 / Hello, Nattapat,

Did I let you know I received all of your work the other day? If not, well…it was, not surprisingly, first-rate on first reading — and I look forward to a second reading soon. Can't wait to see how you and others in the class handle the Blackboard materials I will start sending out for WAITING FOR THE BARBARIANS and everything else (and it's lots) that will follow.

Collegially,

Bob Eidelberg

March 16 / Hello Professor Eidelberg,

Yes I received the notification. Thank you for the kind words. Looking forward to future assignments.

Nattapat

March 19 / Hello Professor Eidelberg,

Here are my thoughts on the several prompts that are due today. The "waiting" of the characters:

1a. The narrator: waiting for the agent from the Empire to leave, waiting for his peaceful life and blissful ignorance to return, waiting to know why he kept the girl for so long, waiting to drown himself in the past rather than act in the present. The form of his waiting includes his increasing visit to The Star (or bird), and spending time washing and sleeping next to the girl. Hunting – or trying to hunt. And long walks accompanied by rumination about life and seriously long thoughts about other's views on him.

1b. The girl: waiting for the next day. Her form of waiting is spending time cooking and cleaning in the kitchen. Getting washed by the narrator and dealing with his curiosities.

1c. The agent from the Empire: waiting for the "truth." Spending his day in lavish luxury before doing his job. Also torturing is his form of waiting.

2. With the quick language lesson from you in this prompt, I feel like the title of the novel is now "waiting for the strangers or outsiders"; however, does that outsider represent the nomadic tribe or the Empire, that is yet to be determined. I say – with a growing headache – it's everyone that is not the narrator himself disrupting his peace of mind. However, our narrator has accepted his "barbarian nature" about going with his feelings rather than trying to understand anything or pretending to know anything, and just accepting things as they come.

3. In consideration of the quote "we have met the enemy and he is us," I believe that the novel hinted at this theme right from the beginning with the imprisonment and torture of the child and grandparent pair in the very beginning of the book. This theme is then gradually given tangible form as our narrator saw the damage done to the girl and later the occupation and ransacking of the town by the new officer. Additionally, on a more personal level, the narrator is also his own worst enemy with his curiosities and fancies leading him down a path of trouble, first with investigating the boy and his grandpa, in addition to collecting the past relics of a by-gone settlement – which he himself knew would cause issues if the Empire were to have found out – and then his continual interaction (but also inaction) towards the girl before returning her to the barbarians, marking the last nail on the coffin to be hammered.

March 24 / Hello Professor Eidelberg,

I am waiting for my virtual math class to be over, so please patiently wait for those pdfs. Sorry for the delay.

Nattapat

March 27 / From Nattapat,

Here is my essay.

March 27 / Hello, Nattapat,

Many thanks, Nattapat, for the early submission on the Charles Dickens novel. I have "great expectations" for it (sorry, couldn't resist). It is irresistible, isn't it?

You will be sending a copy to your groupmates, right?

Collegially,

Bob Eidelberg

March 27 / From Nattapat,

Yes, it is. And yes, I will and did. They will not have to wait for it any longer.

March 29 / Hello Professor Eidelberg,

Sorry for the late submission, hope I didn't keep you waiting – well, the reason is in the journal, so enjoy.

Nattapat

April 9 / Hello Professor Eidelberg,

Hope you are doing well. After checking over the latest post on Blackboard I began to have some doubt as to whether or not I have turned in everything I needed to. Did you receive them? Or, I suppose the question is, are you waiting for any piece from me?

Nattapat

April 14 / Hello, Nattapat,

Four perceptive responses to the questions on THE WIZARD OF OZ — and thanks for the link to Plato!

In that connection, why don't you take a crack at the CW/HW with Patience (in what form?) as a fourth character seeking out the wisdom of the Wizard. Interested?

Collegially,

Bob Eidelberg

April 14 / Hello Professor Eidelberg,

I'm certainly interested, I'll take some time and think about the character a bit more. Please wait patiently (pun intended).

Nattapat

April 14 / Hello, Nattapat,

Great! It's not that I can't wait: I can wait…patiently. With moderation.

Collegially,

Bob Eidelberg

April 14 / Hello Professor Eidelberg,

One upped at my own game. Like I stated before, Golem is a creature made of stone and so is supposed to be patient. However, this particular individual feels that he doesn't have enough patience because he can't sit still for a long time like his kin. Golem then sets on a journey with the gang in the hopes that Oz can give him more patience – along the way he often walks slower than the rest and takes time to enjoy the sights and talks. Especially when everyone else was stressing over when Oz would see them, Golem was mostly fine. Oz would likely give Golem one of those Newton's cradles to keep his mind off the time.

Nattapat

April 14 / From Nattapat,

Here you go Professor Eidelberg. The wait was wicked, but not so much so as the witch of the west – as such I present to you Golem learning to wait like a stone.

April 16 / Hello, Professor Eidelberg, and groupmates,

I hope you are all doing well in this troubling time. Concerning "The Decameron" I have to say my favorite is the Fourth Story. I love the way that Dioneo just began telling this story without the queen having to ask, first of all. It gave me the feeling that she just has this story excitedly in her mind.

Nattapat

April 22 / Hello Professor Eidelberg,

Sitting here, scrolling mindlessly through poems, I realize – I'm not in a mood for poems. The vivid imagery vaporized, the wordplay skimmed, feeling indifferent. I'll try again tomorrow.

Nattapat

April 23 / Hello, Nattapat,

You know, Nattapat, that was a terrific poem you sent me yesterday! If only someone else had written it and it was waiting for you to find it online (as per the assignment to you and your groupmates!).

Collegially,

Bob Eidelberg

May 2 / Hello Professor Eidelberg,

I just went to the post office today to deposit the letter of consent for publication of my writing in our course's book SOME DAY. Please email me once it arrives. I suppose the waiting for next week and the week after would be waiting for your email for my mail from your email.

Nattapat

May 2 / Hello, Nattapat,

Not if I email right now to let you know that I got your email that....... (you know the drill).

But how come you had to go "all the way" to the post office? Is there no "mailbox" on a corner nearer to you in the Bronx than where the Post Office (ta-dah!) Is located?

Collegially,

Bob Eidelberg

P.S. And, oh yes, thanks for the you know what.

May 2 / Hello Professor Eidelberg,

Unfortunately no, the closest place for the I know you know I know what is the present and pleasant post office.

Nattapat

May 7 / Hey Professor Eidelberg,

Looking at Lucky's speech in "Waiting for Godot" was really mind-numbingly interesting that I spent nearly three days thinking it through, but the speeches I wrote for the submission earlier today felt like they were missing something, something representative in the original; right when I was about to throw in the towel – quite literally in this case – this new speech for Lucky luckily came to me. Although I still feel something is missing, I still feel quite lucky to have this shower thought.

Nattapat

PANDEMIC EMAIL SENT THROUGHOUT APRIL 2020

BY INSTRUCTOR ROBERT EIDELBERG
TO HIS HOMEBOUND STUDENTS

Hello, Colleagues,

Although our last off-campus class is not until Thursday, May 7, 2020, I am sending you this – via your personal email rather than via Blackboard – several weeks in advance so that you have plenty of time to work out how you want to "experience" Session #28 through distance learning. There are a lot of options (see them below) and many of them are geared to how you have already experienced and will continue to experience our course. Most important of all, you do NOT have to choose any of the options since the entire session on May 7th is totally and completely optional.

Huh? Or what do I mean by that? What I mean is that whatever you decide to do is "extra credit" toward your final course mark in The Literature of Waiting / English 25146, and many of you will not need extra credit in order to get as your final course mark the same A or A+ that you received as your mid-course mark on March 10. However, some of you will want to do a certain amount of extra credit to try to move an A- to a solid A or an A to an A+. (There were no passing mid-course grades below A- on March 10; there were, however, two "F" failures.)

Others of you, because of the anxiety surrounding the coronavirus pandemic and its attendant physical issues, psychological issues, and related economic issues, have slipped noticeably – not in the high quality of the work you have produced but in its quantity (missing – and continuing to miss – several academic and creative pieces of writing that showed you had kept up with the assigned reading, including your independent reading within a group of your colleagues).

Important note: if you are in this just-mentioned category, you may NOT select the option dealing with Eugene O'Neill's play THE ICEMAN COMETH. I have eliminated this work as required reading for all of us (for me, too) because, in my opinion, in these worrisome times it is too dark a work, too nihilistic a work, too hopeless a work for those of you currently having a difficult time coping with the effects of the pandemic on your hearts, minds, and souls.

Though this lengthy-to-read and quite-long play to sit through works far better on the stage than on the page (I have seen three star performers in three first-rate productions of THE ICEMAN COMETH in my lifetime, and at least two of them are readily available to most of you on YouTube), it would be highly insensitive of me at this point in our teacher-student-colleague relationship to suggest it (let alone require it) to those of you who have enough on your plate and on your mind: you certainly don't need any additional stressor.

So, look over all of the options you have and decide which you will complete by NO LATER THAN May 7 (the official last session of our course). Depending on where you see yourself (re-read all the above paragraphs!), choose one, or two, or none. If you want to run your thoughts about this by me, write me at our course email glamor62945@mypacks. net and I will get back to you right away.

(Note from the instructor to the readers of the book HEY, PROFESSOR: By the numbers, the following extra credit options were in fact selected and submitted by students: 1, 2, 3, 4, 7, 9.)

1. Only if you can emotionally handle this famous downer of a "waiting and expecting" play: read (or see on YouTube, or do both) THE ICEMAN COMETH – and then write Mr. Eidelberg a detailed letter as to why it would be, post-pandemic, a good idea – or not – to include O'Neill's play as required reading in "The Literature of Waiting" course in the spring of 2021. (You might also want to consider it as one of the class's independent reading works that a group of 4 or 5 students sign up for.)
2. Write a dialogue that two characters (each from a different work of literature experienced this term) could have in person, or

by phone, or by text, or by letter; you may include one other character if you want to or need to; this third character can be from a third work of lit or from one of the original two. Please keep the length of this mini-play to under four single-spaced typed pages since I already have from Fawzi Saleh – have some of you heard about this? – a piece of writing (which he calls SYNTHESI) along similar lines that runs 18 pages (!) and includes something like 33 characters (!) from almost all of the literature we studied up to the mid-point in the course.

3. Write a prose piece or a poem or a playlet (mini-play) that could have as its title "Endurance." Or "Still Waiting." Or "The Waiting Room."

4. Write a prose piece or a poem that could have as its title "Living Is a Kind of Waiting to Dying."

5. Write a contemporary short story that could be included as one of the tales in Giovanni Boccaccio's THE DECAMERON.

6. Read one of the other five works of "waiting" literature not read by your group, and write an essay in which you try to persuade Mr. Eidelberg to make that book required reading for the whole class in the spring of 2021.

7. Write an essay that explains the nature and workings of "The Theater of the Absurd" using as examples WAITING FOR GODOT, THE DUMB WAITER, and, if you read it, ROSENCRANZ AND GUILDENSTERN ARE DEAD.

8. Create a board game (like MONOPOLY) that has as its trade-marked name THE WAITING GAME complete with board, rules, pieces that get moved around the board, chance cards (that get picked up on the throw of the dice and which dictate opportunities and/or setbacks for the player), and so forth.

9. Write an essay in which you explore how the philosophical meaning of "waiting" – in literature and in life – has changed for you (or not) as a result of taking this course on "The Literature of Waiting."

10. View the film WAIT UNTIL DARK on YouTube.

Collegially,

Bob Eidelberg

Liala is a graduating senior who lives on Staten Island and commutes to Hunter College by ferry, bus, and subway. She is majoring in psychology and minoring in English and thinks she might become either a psychologist or a writer. Relatively quiet in class during most of our on-campus sessions, Liala showed me just how good a writer she was when our course went into distance learning and Liala's insights into the "waiting" literature under study could take only written form.

Unfortunately, Liala was one of the several students in our class who wound up testing positive for Covid-19 after distance learning began. She recovered, but Liala felt she needed all of May and much of June to take the course on her own and at her own pace and strength – and so she accepted my offer of an Incomplete grade on May 11 and lots of extra credit and replacement work in order to earn the high letter grade she wanted to graduate Hunter with. Liala became "complete" on July 1 with a final grade of "A."

Portrait of On-Campus Liala

January 31 / Hello,

My name is Liala (Lie - lah). I registered late for the course, which was why I hadn't attended class previously and have missed the first two sessions. I checked Blackboard's assignment section but I did not see anything and cannot find the syllabus either. Could you please explain what assignments you need from me? Hope I am not too far behind!

Thanks, and sorry for any inconvenience!

Liala

January 31 / Hello, Liala,

Thanks for getting back to me. I will catch you up next class on Tuesday (no worries!) – but it would help me to do that if you could meet me twenty minutes early outside our classroom – HW404 – at 5:15. Otherwise, see whether my third Blackboard announcement posting helps you get a handle on some things and a head start on others. (Blackboard is always a few days behind in its postings for students who register late for a course.)

Collegially,

Bob Eidelberg

February 1 / Hi Professor,

I can definitely meet you before class and I will go check out Blackboard!

Thanks,

Liala

February 25 / Hi Professor,

I was trying to go do this assignment but I was unhappy with the way my timeline for the novel 'Waiting" came out. I was working all weekend so I feel like I didn't have enough time to complete it properly along with all of my other assignments. Is there any way you can extend the due date? Also, I think I sent my assignments to the wrong email last week.

Best,

Liala

February 25 / Hello,

Sorry, Liala, but however much of the timeline for one "Waiting" character you have completed will determine which group you are in during tonight's class. Better some of an imperfect timeline than nothing; otherwise, you will not be able to function at all in the group and turning in a partial or complete timeline after tonight's class will serve no purpose instructionally.

Collegially,

Bob Eidelberg

Portrait of Distance-Learner Liala

March 19 / Hi Professor,

Hope you're indoors and safe. Just emailing you because I believe Michael and Nicole are in my "Age of Innocence" group. Can you provide me with their emails and let me know when to contact them? As well as what will the group assignment be and when will it be due now that it will not be a group oral presentation in front of the rest of the class.

Thanks,

Liala

March 19 / Hi Professor,

Attached is the "Waiting for the Barbarians" assignment based on prompts 1 and 7.

Best,

Liala

March 19 / Hello, Liala,

You should have gotten all the contact info by today from your groupmate Michael; let's give it another day or so and if you don't have it by Saturday, let me know. As to the collaborative assignment, all the info about the group aspect will be coming to you all in about a week (there is also an individual component that I will let everyone know about at that time).

Collegially,

Bob Eidelberg

March 28 / Hello Selected Colleagues,

I hope you are physically and psychologically well during these stressful times since March 10, but I have noticed that since the start of distance learning you have not been fully involved in the work of our course as detailed in the Calendar of Sessions that you have in your possession (for Sessions #14 through #18, in particular) as well as in the changes, additions, and subtractions to the required reading and writing listed under those sections as detailed in six Blackboard announcements posted by me on a regular basis.

Besides from the fact that all CUINY faculty are now being asked to report the names of such students to, in your cases, Hunter College, I would like to reach out to you once again before I do anything in an official capacity that might jeopardize your status at Hunter. (Not so incidentally, I have sent personal email requests to several of you for pdf attachments of your first-rate pieces of creative writing done while we all were meeting together as a class on campus and those emails were neither complied with nor acknowledged.)

Seriously, I do hope you are reasonably okay, but I would feel a lot better if I knew that directly from you.

I hope you will respond to this email within the next day or so.

Collegially,

Bob Eidelberg

March 28 / Hello, Selected Colleagues,

I hope you and your loved ones are doing well; I have a favor to ask of you in these chaotic times. I would like to include in our course's book SOME DAY the first-rate work you did (a 95 or higher mark) on the several creative writing pieces you wrote earlier in the semester and up to the end of on-campus instruction. So, if you can, please send me within the next few days a pdf of any of those pieces that you would like to be considered for publication, such as the Kate Croy found poem, the letter to a friend inspired by a song, the coda to THE DUMB WAITER, the changes you made in the vignettes to WAITING FOR LEFTY, and especially, your "How to Be a Waiter" piece.

Many thanks. Stay well and calm, sane and productive, caring and kind to others.

Collegially,

Bob Eidelberg

March 28 / Hi Professor,

I am writing to you late but I'm feeling less weak today. Basically, I've had a fever for the past two days as well as a cough. I've had headaches and I'm perpetually tired. Since I seem to have symptoms of the coronavirus I have been self-quarantining. I am also trying to get tested, so if I do I will update you on the results. I'm sorry if I am late on giving in any assignments, I hope you will give me an extension.

Best,

Liala

March 28 / Hello, Liala,

Of course you have whatever extension is needed given what your health concerns are. I wish you well with getting tested and following up on the medical advice you receive. Keep in touch when you can. All the best!

Collegially,

Bob Eidelberg

April 6 / Hello, Liala,

Hoping you are doing better — actually, well. Did you wind up getting tested?

Collegially,

Bob Eidelberg

April 7 / Hi Professor,

After weeks of being sick I was finally able to get tested for the coronavirus and tested positive. I'm just starting to really recover and am getting cleared to get back to my classes. Please let me know what I missed and what you need from me as of right now. That being said I hope you are well and staying safe.

Best,

Liala

April 8 / Hello, Liala,

I'm so sorry to hear this news that you seemed to have been expecting but, on the other hand, I'm so glad you went ahead and got tested so that you could take care. From what I think I know about you as a young adult, it seems that you will stay smart and do whatever it takes to get well.

Is there anything I or your class colleagues or your groupmates for THE AGE OF INNOCENCE project can do to assist you in this? Do you have any thoughts about how you want to proceed with any of the recent or future work of the course?

Please stay in touch — and get fully better in record time!

Collegially,

Bob Eidelberg

April 9 / Hello, groupmates for the project on the novel THE AGE OF INNOCENCE,

Are any of you in the process of finishing up on your personal essay about THE AGE OF INNOCENCE?

All of the five other groups have fairly fully reported in and their work has been reproduced by me for what will be Chapter 15 of our course's book SOME DAY.

Weird — but I don't have a word in that chapter on the Edith Wharton novel, which is not only a literary shame but an inexplicable class anomaly!

So, would ALL OF YOU get back to me one way or the other on the answer to the question of whether any of you is finishing up an essay?

Collegially,

Bob Eidelberg

April 15 / Hi Professor,

Thank you for the well wishes and concern, Professor. My groupmates have also been patient with me and for that I am grateful. Sick or not, it seems we are all struggling during these hard times. I am happy to say that after taking extra time I finally completed the assignment. Attached here is my essay on "The Age of Innocence." Sorry if it is a little lengthy ... I guess I had a lot to say. In the coming weeks, I hope to catch up on all of the work I missed.

Best,

Liala

April 15 / Hello, Liala,

You did have a lot to say – and you said it quite well and convincingly. Welcome back!

Collegially,

Bob Eidelberg

April 15 / From Liala,

Thank you, professor, but unfortunately, I am going through housing instability right now and have been displaced from my home. I am trying to get by but it is very difficult for me to complete my school work at this very moment. I am concerned about the semester ending in two weeks and the fact that I have not been able to be as productive as I need to be. I am trying to get back on my feet by working two jobs and would love to finish off the semester properly but I'm not sure I can manage it right now. Is there any way I can get an extension for my final assignments?

April 15 / Hello, Liala,

So sorry to hear about what you are still going through. Would you like to consider an extension to the end of June and I would enter, in mid-May, a grade of "Incomplete" that I could then on July 1 change to a passing letter grade?

Collegially,

Bob Eidelberg

April 16 / From Liala,

Yes, that would be all the difference. Thank you so much, Professor Eidelberg.

Best,

Liala

April 17 / Hello, Liala,

You are welcome, Liala.

So on May 11, I will enter an "Incomplete" for your final course grade and then, throughout the rest of May and into June, I will be looking for the missing and/or replacement work you will be sending me for reading and evaluating and numerical grading.

Please don't stress out!

Collegially,

Bob Eidelberg

May 14 / Hi Professor,

Hope you are well. I am sorry that I have not responded to your last emails until now... have been working nearly 80 hours per week. I attached the signed consent form along with some of my pieces that I wish to include in SOME DAY. Looking forward to reading it once it gets published.

Best,

Liala

May 22 / Hello, Colleagues for whom I have already entered an "INC" (Incomplete) on the grade roster:

I am concerned that I have started to receive some missing and/or replacement work from ONLY 2 of the 9 of you that I have an agreement with, and I am already under some pressure to justify to Hunter College such a high number of INC grades in one course (fully a third of the class).

So, all nine of you, please start sending me work that I can point to as evidence that you are actually busy working right now to upheld your end of our agreement (regardless of the actual end date that we agreed upon a few weeks ago). I would hate to have the whole arrangement for all of you jeopardized by my inability to document that work is being sent to me by all of you on a fairly regular basis over the next weeks.

Thank you for your understanding.

Collegially,

Bob Eidelberg

May 23 / Hi Professor,

Attached are some of the assignments from Sessions 21 and 23. Also, an extra credit piece, a short play (as you know from my course work, professor, I like creating short plays) I call "Nail Polish," in which a troubled marriage finally breaks up under the stress of the coronavirus epidemic. Its closing words are: "I can't see through the blurring of my eyes. Feeling a wet droplet hit my hand, I look down and find every single one of my freshly polished nails ruined."

Hope you are in good health and are remaining safe.

Best,

Liala

June 18 / Hello to the Four English 25146 "Incomplete" Colleagues Who Have Until June 30 to Submit Their Missing Homework Assignments and Replacement Work,

I hope you four are relatively well and working on your assignments relatively diligently.

As I've mentioned previously, on the first of July I must officially contact Hunter College and inform them of which letter grade your Incomplete is to be changed to. Since I have not received much work from some of you in recent weeks (despite my stressing the importance of your sending me each piece as you complete it so that I have time to read it carefully and evaluate it fairly), I am concerned that I will be inundated with lots of writing from the four of you in the last three days of June.

Here's how I feel about that: with so little time for me to read and evaluate that much work, it is highly unlikely that any of you would wind up with a mark of A- or A. If that is not an actual concern for you, I would have no problem entering a mark of either B or B+ (depending) for you on next Monday, June 22, based on my record of all that you have done and done well both in our thirteen on-campus classes and since distance learning began after March 10. If that works for you, please let me know right away.

And if you still want the time until June 30 to work at home some more to get a final course grade of A- or A, then you MUST send me something substantial that you have recemntly written for the course by that same date — next Monday, June 22.

If you have any questions about any of this, of course email them to me immediately.

Collegially,

Bob Eidelberg

July 1 / Hello, Laila,

Just wanted to let you know that based on your meeting our July 1 deadline with a sufficient number of quality pieces of written work (made-up missing assignments, replacement assignments, extra credit pieces), I have formally requested Hunter College to change your Incomplete to a final letter grade of "A" in The Literature of Waiting course.

Congratulations on what was a far from easy or easily assumed academic achievement in these troubled times. Have a stress-free, healthy, and happy summer!

Collegially,

Bob Eidelberg

July 2 / Thank you so much, Professor,

It was a pleasure having your class and working with someone so considerate, kind, knowledgeable, and interesting! This class exposed me to some great works of literature and came at such a fitting time that the experience was truly unique, and I would say unforgettable. I'm sure your future students will enjoy the course even more while (hopefully) taking it in person.

Best wishes,

Liala

Michael is a senior (hoping to graduate Hunter College this semester) who lives in the borough of Brooklyn and commutes by subway to Hunter's campus in Manhattan. Michael is majoring in German and minoring in English, but he did not indicate any career plans on his Colleague Profile the first day of our course.

The narrative arc of our email correspondence during distance learning (there was no real distance teaching on my part, apparently) could be considered emblematic of the real-life adjustment problems posed by distance learning for many of today's urban college students. With all the best of intentions, hopes, plans, and promises during our course's three months of distance learning, Michael wound up emailing me little more than his "kind regards."

Portrait of On-Campus and Distance-Learner Michael

March 10 / Dear Professor Eidelberg,

I hope this email finds you well. I have been feeling sick the past couple of days with a runny nose and throat pain. As a result, I felt that it would be the most responsible option to not come to class this afternoon. I have attached the assignments that were due in the body of the email below. Thank you!

Best regards,

Michael

March 19 / Hi Professor Eidelberg,

I hope this finds you well and that you are staying safe and sane despite the isolation. I attached the assignment for today's class in this email. Please let me know if you have any questions!

Kind regards,

Michael

March 25 / Hello Selected Colleagues,

I hope you are physically and psychologically well during these stressful times since March 10, but I have noticed that since the start of distant learning you have not been fully involved in the work of our course as detailed in the Calendar of Sessions that you have in your possession (for Sessions #14 through #18, in particular) as well as in the changes, additions, and subtractions to the required reading and writing listed under those sections as detailed in six Blackboard announcements posted by me on a regular basis.

Besides from the fact that all CUINY faculty are now being asked to report the names of such students to, in your cases, Hunter College, I would like to reach out to you once again before I do anything in an official capacity that might jeopardize your status at Hunter. (Not so incidentally, I have sent personal email requests to several of you for pdf attachments of your first-rate pieces of creative writing done while we all were meeting together as a class on campus and those emails were neither complied with nor acknowledged.)

Seriously, I do hope you are reasonably okay, but I would feel a lot better if I knew that directly from you.

I hope you will respond to this email within the next day or so.

Collegially,

Bob Eidelberg

March 26 / Dear Professor Eidelberg,

I hope this email finds you well. Thank you for reaching out and expressing your concern. This transition has been a little of a challenge for me – I've been trying to adjust to feeling a lot more anxiety after being laid off from my job as a waiter and getting used to spending much more time at home, where I live with my brother, his wife, and their (quite rambunctious) three-year-old son. I am used to being able to do my coursework in the library or at cafes and I am still adjusting to having to do the majority of my work at home. As a result, I have fallen a little behind in my coursework.

I do apologize for not asking this sooner, but I was wondering if it might be possible to have the Recalibration Period to get caught up on my work for this class. I know that you do not normally accept late work and that you have already given extensions as is, but given the exceptional circumstances, it would be incredibly helpful to have the next few days in order to get back on top of everything. I promise that I will complete all of my work over the weekend and then submit the rest of the coursework for the semester on time. If this is something you think you might be able to agree to, please let me know. I appreciate your patience and understanding during this time.

Sincerely,

Michael

May 3 / Hello, Selected Colleagues,

It's been a while since I have heard from you either by a response to an email of mine, a Blackboard request, or a significant number of homework assignments turned in (even late), and I am concerned about your physical and mental health and your anxiety status during these worrisome times.

Also, I don't know whether you are doing any of the currently required reading in our "Literature of Waiting" course and are planning to send in some of the assigned written work (and/or optional replacement work) to me by this Thursday, May 7th, when our course officially has its last "session," but I do know that I will have to enter a course letter grade for you in the following weeks.

Some of your colleagues in our class have already opted for an arrangement in which I enter a grade of "Incomplete" on May 11th and then, after sufficient quality work has been turned in by a given date (June 1st, for example), I officially change the "Incomplete" to a passing grade of at least B+ (but higher letter grades are still possible).

Others have told me that such an extension (even to July 1st) would not work for them in their current stressful situation and that they would prefer that I give them an actual final passing grade on May 11th (one based on the numerical grade earned at the mid-point in the course on March

12th, plus or minus the quantity and quality of the work done since we all started to shelter in place at home.

I would appreciate your giving your options in this difficult situation some thought and your getting back to me as soon as possible by return email with how you would like for both of us to proceed.

Many thanks – and please be well and stay as healthily productive as you can.

Collegially,

Bob Eidelberg

May 6 / Dear Professor Eidelberg,

I hope this email finds you well and that you and your loved ones are safe and healthy. First, I just want to apologize for my lack of communication this past couple of months. I know that I dropped the ball considerably in not reaching out for more help after my initial email to you some weeks back, and I sincerely apologize for not having done so. This has been a really difficult time for me, as it has been for many, and I have been really struggling with managing my anxiety and stress and finding the capacity or motivation to do my schoolwork. That said, I take complete responsibility for not being more proactive and a better advocate for myself.

I do, however, feel like I am now in a place where I can finish the work that I missed this semester. I've worked out a schedule and now have access to some quiet and solitary hours during the day where I can work on the schoolwork that I've had trouble finishing. If it might be possible to take an incomplete when you enter grades, I am very confident that I could finish the remainder of the work by June 1st and hopefully finish the course with a passing grade. I will be sure to communicate more regularly until then if I do need more help. If that sounds like something that you might be able to agree to, I would be incredibly grateful for the opportunity to finish the semester on a better note.

Please feel free to let me know either way. Again, my sincerest apologies for sending this email so late in the semester. If there is one thing I have learned from this semester it is to be more comfortable asking for help when I need it. I appreciate your patience, understanding, and flexibility throughout.

Kind regards,

Michael

May 15 / Hello, Colleagues for whom I have already entered an "INC" (Incomplete) on the grade roster:

I am concerned that I have started to receive some missing and/or replacement work from ONLY 2 of the 9 of you that I have an agreement with, and I am already under some pressure to justify to Hunter College such a high number of INC grades in one course (fully a third of the class).

So, all nine of you, please start sending me work that I can point to as evidence that you are actually busy working right now to upheld your end of our agreement (regardless of the actual end date that we agreed upon a few weeks ago). I would hate to have the whole arrangement for all of you jeopardized by my inability to document that work is being sent to me by all of you on a fairly regular basis over the next weeks.

Thank you for your understanding.

Collegially,

Bob Eidelberg

May 18 / Hi Professor Eidelberg,

I hope this finds you well. My apologies for the delayed response. I have attached to this email the consent form for my written work to be published in our course's book SOME DAY and will be following up with makeup work in the coming days. Thank you again for your patience and understanding! I really appreciate everything that you have done in order to allow me and other students to complete the course!

Kind regards,

Michael

June 5 / Hello, Michael,

I hope things are not too terrible with you but I must admit that I am concerned since you have again lost touch with me (and not responded to any of my recent emails to you).

Here's the situation I'm in right now by not knowing the situation you're in. Not only did I not get those assignments you said were on the way but what should show as an Incomplete for you on the online grade roster mistakenly shows an A- (the mark you might very well receive if you complete your contract with me). That A- cannot stand, but for now I am not going to contact Hunter about this posting error — that is, until I hear from you. For all I know, you might be interested in the pass/fail option of CR (do you know about that?) or be okay with a B- to be entered by the end of next week based on all the work of yours I've received and evaluated since the start of the course.

But until I hear from you (it's got to be soon!) I will not take any action — but I truly need to hear from you.

Collegially,

Bob Eidelberg

Note from the Instructor: I made one last attempt to learn what Michael's at-home and at-work distance learning situation was (remember, he had written me on May 6, the day before the last session of our course on "The Literature of Waiting," that, having worked out a schedule, he was very confident that he could finish the course work by June 1 and earn a passing letter grade). More than a full month after that email, I decided to telephone Michael on the personal cellphone number he had listed as a real contact number for him on Day 1 of the course ("the one you regularly check and return calls from"). Up to this point I had telephoned just two other anxiety-ridden students during the three months my students and I lived out and survived our common conundrum of distance learning, and only one of them relatively successfully. Also, truth be told, I'm not a telephone person.)

So, on the morning of June 8, I telephoned Michael; it had been fully three days since I had sent him the above email (and not heard from him "soon," which is to say, at all), and when his "you have reached" recorded message came on, I left a detailed oral version of the key points I had made in that email of June 5. I did not get a call back.

On the afternoon of June 10, I contacted Hunter College and requested a correction to the erroneous posting for Michael of an A- instead of the INC for Incomplete, and when asked to enter the correct final course letter grade, I decided that the story of Michael's on-campus and distance learning experience in "The Literature of Waiting" had come to its conclusion: I gave Michael the B- grade I had run by him in the email and for the reasons stated; it was a drop of three letter grades from his mid-course mark of an A-, and exactly three months to the day later.

Later that same afternoon (did you think the story, though concluded, was over?), Michael sent me the following email; it reads like a direct response to my email of June 5, without any reference to the message I had left on his cellphone.

June 10 / Hi Professor Eidelberg,

I hope this email finds you well. I really appreciate you reaching out to me before taking action with the college. This is the last grade that I need to take care of before I graduate and I am (rather desperately) trying to find a new job before my pandemic unemployment insurance runs out, which has taken up a lot of my time. I would be happy to receive any credit I can for this course. I really appreciate your understanding and patience throughout this past semester and hope you enjoy your summer. Please let me know if you have any questions or concerns for me.

Kind regards,

Michael

Fawzi is an upper junior who lives in the borough of Queens, New York, and commutes to college by subway. Majoring in biochemistry, he is undecided about his career goal but does have decided opinions on expressing his ideas almost always in writing and almost never in class. (Fawzi did allow me, reluctantly, to coax him into playing the role of Ben in front of the class one day – but it was the "Ben" that he had created for an imaginative coda to Harold Pinter's theater-of-the-absurd one-act play THE DUMB WAITER.)

The shutdown of the Hunter College campus after our thirteenth class session on March 10 and the consequent inception of distance learning worked very much in Fawzi's letter grade favor since it flipped the credit emphasis of our course on "The Literature of Waiting" from informed and insightful oral participation in class to informed and insightful academic writing at home.

However, during both halves of the course, Fawzi always exceled as a prolific writer of very imaginative pieces spun off from the literature we were studying. His unsolicited 18-page magnum opus, which he called "Synthesi," combined 33 characters from 12 of the course's pieces of literature – and I used it, by itself, as the concluding chapter to the course's published book SOME DAY: The Literature of Waiting – A Creative Writing Course With Times on Its Hands.

Portrait of On-Campus Fawzi

February 28 / Hello Professor Eidelberg,

I apologize for not emailing you earlier. After all this time has passed, I forgot what I was going to email you about. Perhaps it was about the "Dumb Waiter" coda presentation, but all I'll say about that is that I'll try to do better in future presentations.

To not let this email (and your time) go to waste, I'll leave you with a one-more-thing.

Yesterday, many people raised some excellent points in class about the waiting done by Lin, Manna, and Shuyu in the novel "Waiting." One of them stood out though, and it was Shanya's comment about Lin. She said that at the end of the story, she concluded that Lin was in love with himself. She explained this by stating that throughout the book, we are simply waiting for Lin to get bored.

I thought this was an interesting interpretation of the ending or Lin's waiting. I would like to politely disagree because I don't think Lin is at fault here. Lin was never bored of Shuyu, he did not desire her in the first place. And because he worked in the city, he did not spend enough time with her to ever develop a bond with her. Then there is Manna. She is the one who started the affair and also the one who escalated it to a marriage. And Lin wanted to leave not out of boredom but because of their frustrating relationship. Manna could not balance the responsibilities of caring for the twins and being a wife to Lin. This took a toll on her physical and mental health, and made their relationship get worse and worse, to the point where Lin simply wanted to escape.

In my view, toward the end, Lin was not in love with himself, Shuyu or Manna. For himself, we see him occasionally talking to himself. Almost always, his alternate ego is attacking him and making him doubt himself. So he has a pessimistic view of himself (and probably the world) so he definitely does not love himself. For Shuyu, she is so caring and obedient, both throughout the book and toward the end, that this turns off Lin. He wants to love someone who has an authentic personality. Shuyu is not like that at all. As a matter of fact, she barely appears in the book enough for the reader to truly understand her. In Book 1, Chapter 11, she appears as little more than a slave caring for Lin. In Book 2, she does not appear at all. In Book 3, Chapter 1 she briefly chats with the nurses and seems more like a child than a married woman. Finally, in Chapter 12, we see her crying of joy because Lin says he will return to her, but this does not reveal anything new about Shuyu. And him returning to her does not indicate that he loves or will ever love her. Lin loving Shuyu is like a Master falling in love with their slave because their slave toils for them. It does not happen, and I don't think it will ever happen in Lin and Shuyu's case. He might return to her, but he will never love her. With Manna, he only loved her as a friend. He was lonely at the hospital and he wanted someone to spend time with. He found that in Manna, she was beautiful and he liked being with her. But his love did not go beyond friendship. He never wanted to get married or even have children with her. These were things that Manna forced onto him, and he reluctantly obeyed so he wouldn't lose her.

I'm interested in hearing what you think about my thoughts. Also, if I have interpreted Shanya's comment about Lin loving himself or being bored incorrectly, please let me know and explain to me what she means.

Sincerely,

Fawzi

Portrait of Distance-Learner Fawzi

After "Synthesi" arrived unsolicited in our course's email inbox / Hello, Fawzi,

This is one of the finest pieces of imaginative writing I have read in decades of teaching. Amazingly, you anticipated a favorite end-of-course creative writing assignment of mine that asks all students to do a piece of imaginative writing that involves characters from at least three of the works of literature studied and places them in narrative and dramatic interaction with one another in a way that brings to life the major theme of the course.

Your eighteen-page piece should stay just between us for now because if other students got to experience it at this point in the term, I fear that instead of serving as a model it would frighten your colleagues into total inaction and lots of blank pages.

I guess you knew what you were asking about — and for — when you made that request that all oral participation group and front-of-the-room assignments for the class become written assignments for you!

Collegially,

Bob Eidelberg

March 16 / Hello, Professor,

I had no prior knowledge that our end-of-the-semester assignment would be this – and I will not tell anyone about it.

Attached is my "Telephone Call" assignment that continues the Dorothy Parker short story.

Sincerely,

Fawzi

March 20 / Hello Professor Eidelberg,

Here are the questions for Thursday's assignment, I apologize for the tardiness.

March 22 / Hello Professor Eidelberg,

I will send my CW pdf from my gmail because it doesn't seem to go through with my Hunter email.

Sincerely,

Fawzi

March 22 / Dear Professor Eidelberg,

Attached is the "Dumb Waiter" coda that I wrote.

Sincerely,

Fawzi

April 1 / Hello, Selected Colleagues,

This email may look like a duplicate of one of the ones I've sent out recently, but actually it is a new and very specific request asking that you put onto a clickable pdf (if you can) the first-rate creative piece of writing you did a while back inspired by one of your entries in your personal waiting journal.

I have read, evaluated, and graded (quite highly) the originals you submitted around the 9th and 10th of March (just before the close of the campus), but in order for me to use these terrific pieces of writing in our course's book SOME DAY, I must have them re-sent to me on a pdf by no later than this Sunday, April 5 (if humanly possible!).

In any case, please respond to this email acknowledging that you have received this request of mine.

Many thanks.

Be well, stay calm, be kind, stay sane.

Collegially,

Bob Eidelberg

April 2 / Hello Professor Eidelberg,

I've attached the pdf for the HW that was due on 3/31. I apologize for the lateness.

Sincerely,

Fawzi

April 2 / Hello, Fawzi,

My plan is to publish your phenomenal story SYNTHESI as the concluding chapter to our course's book SOME DAY. The attached pdf page would be how the story is introduced.

Did I miss any characters or works of lit you make use of? Do I have the first-mentioned order of the works of lit correct? (Don't count the characters because I doubt we'd agree!)

Kudos on your remarkable achievement — you are some synthesizer; you are some writer!

Collegially,

Bob Eidelberg

April 2 / Hello Professor Eidelberg,

I'm glad you liked the CW assignment. The truth is, that is the shortened version of the story. I don't know if you noticed, but the stories at the end were a bit rushed. For instance, Ben from "The Dumb Waiter" barely had any dialogue and the characters from "Waiting for Lefty" were nonexistent. Originally, I had planned to make them interact with Lin, my main character (from the novel "Waiting"), and with each other and contribute to the overall story, which would have been 10 additional pages at the very least. Unfortunately, I had other coursework and thus could not complete it.

The attached pdf looks very good, thank you for writing it.

Sincerely,

Fawzi

April 2 / Hello, Fawzi,

I did notice — but I must tell you that I think that intuitively you did the better thing. Not only is the shorter version more readable, but I thought that how you intentionally "framed" the characters from WAITING FOR LEFTY was a terrific touch. Not a word of dialogue spoken, but very effective visualization of characters in crisis.

Collegially,

Bob Eidelberg

P.S.: Is the reference to "a writer" and the magazine "The Saturday Evening Post" also a particular allusion from our class discussions of "waiting" literature?

April 3 / From Fawzi,

The writer is Russell Baker from his memoir "Growing Up" and the reference to the magazine comes from his job delivering them as a young boy.

April 7 / Dear Wardah (one of Fawzi's three groupmates reading Daniel Defoe's novel ROBINSON CRUSOE),

The three themes you attribute to this book are interesting. Survival, you say, refers to overcoming fears and obstacles in life. This is an important life skill to have, and surviving on an island is perhaps the best way to convey it, so I agree that readers would benefit from reading this book in that respect.

Self-sufficiency ties in to survival; after all, those that survive often are independent, they can take care of themselves, so it goes without saying that this book also teaches that. Finally, there is spirituality. I think that readers will learn that it is a process and that they must awaken their spiritual side by themselves. Overall, I agree with all the themes you identify in this book.

Sincerely,

Fawzi

April 8 / Hello, Fawzi,

Thanks for copying me your reaction to Wardah's piece on ROBINSON CRUSOE. Has she gotten yours yet?

Collegially,

Bob Eidelberg

April 10 / Hello, Fawzi,

Thanks for the rather well-argued "no" to ROBINSON CRUSOE. Your piece will really liven up the discussion of it in our course's book SOME DAY.

Collegially,

Bob Eidelberg

P.S. Have you been able to put your hands on a copy of your WAITING marriage counseling session CW/HW so you can send it to me as a link?

May 2 / Dear Professor Eidelberg,

I would like to receive an Incomplete and hand in assignments on June 28.

Also, can I email you my consent form? I've never mailed a letter and would rather avoid it because I'm busy with my finals.

Sincerely,

Fawzi

May 2 / Dear Professor Eidelberg,

Thanks for honoring my request (though not for June 28). I will submit the assignments for Sessions 25-28 by June 1st.

Attached is the consent form.

Sincerely,

Fawzi

June 1 (at 3:58 am) / From Fawzi,

Part One: Read WAITING FOR GODOT straight through, and as you read and intellectually, psychologically, emotionally, and aesthetically react to the "waiting" experience you are having, keep a sequenced list of questions you find yourself wanting to ask (and maybe even get answers for) and would ask if we were going on to discuss the play together in an actual (not sort of virtual) classroom with all our learning and teaching colleagues present.

List of personal questions I want to ask:

1. *Why does he call Estragon "your highness"?*
2. *Why was Estragon beaten?*
3. *Why is the Bible talk so confusing?*
4. *Why are they waiting for Godot?*
5. *What's with the hanging scene?*
6. *What is the point of this play?*

Fawzi decides to answer all of Mr. Eidelberg's "think-about-only" questions (and so gets a bunch of extra credit):

1. Why did everyone (everyone!) I mentioned my then prospective "waiting lit" course to immediately (immediately!) respond with: "What besides WAITING FOR GODOT do you plan for the class to read and study?" (No, I don't only associate with English teachers.)

It is, possibly, the most famous play of the 20ᵗʰ century and has lots of waiting incorporated into it (like the random conversations to pass the time and the mentioning that they have to keep waiting for Godot).

2. Why does it make sense that you, Mr. Teacher of Literature, would end your course on "The Literature of Waiting" with WAITING FOR GODOT rather than start the course with it or teach it somewhere in the middle of the term?

Perhaps "save the best for last" kind of idea, although it's also very long. Starting off with this is probably not a good idea because many students might drop the course (assuming it is too rigorous because of how long this play is).

3. Why are there so many cartoons out there that allude to – nay, directly reference – the play WAITING FOR GODOT (particularly cartoons from "The New Yorker" magazine – want to see my folder)?

The play touches on so many themes and has so much content that it is easy to pluck out lines between characters that convey a specific idea. And because it is a tragicomedy, it can be used for both comical cartoons as well as more serious ones.

4. Who is Godot – and why is anyone at all waiting for him, her, it, them?

Godot, in my opinion, refers to god. The characters are waiting for god to give them some type of order or command, so as to give them a purpose to do something.

5. Is "Godot" pronounced "Guh-dough," with the greater stress on the second syllable or is it pronounced "God-oh," with the greater stress on the first syllable (both pronunciations are out there)? Beckett has answered this question, but does it really matter how the name "Godot" is pronounced?

In my opinion it does because I view Godot as a god, and I'm not sure why someone would pronounce it as "dough," but if they do, it removes the idea of god in the play, which is not good because I think god is at the heart of this play.

6. Does all this waiting matter? And does it matter who is doing the waiting – who they are, how different or alike they are, that there are two of them of the same gender and not three or more in varying combinations? Why not one "waiter"? And, while we're at it, is Godot doing any waiting?

The characters never get to meet Godot, so their waiting for him was fruitless. However, for the audience, this waiting gave them a play to watch, so it is necessary for them. I think the details of the characters are important because they shape how the audience interprets the characters. I think gender is important because if the waiters for women, I personally would not read the play. For some reason, reading a play about women waiting is just not appealing. I don't know why, it's just how I feel. I think the number of the characters is also very important. Two characters is best because it keeps the dialogue simple (it's back and forth, easy to follow). With three or four, it becomes a bit more challenging, as it did for me when Pozzo and Lucky entered into the dialogue (though more so Pozzo, because Lucky barely spoke). I actually would have preferred if the dialogue had stayed between Estragon and Vladimir, as that was easier and more interesting to read, in my opinion. Just one waiter is not sufficient because then there is no dialogue. Sure a character can talk to themselves, but that is just a bit weird (thus unappealing). Assuming Godot is god, no, he does not do any waiting. Waiting only happens to mortals.

7. Have the following authors of recently published illustrated children's books read their Beckett? In WHAT ARE YOU WAITING FOR?, Scott Menchin has a larger animal of one species converse with a smaller animal of another species:
"What are you doing up so early?"
"I'm waiting."
"What are you waiting for?"
"Wouldn't you like to know."
And in Kevin Henkes' illustrated children's book WAITING, a pig with an umbrella is waiting for the rain, a bear with a kite is waiting for the wind, but a rabbit with stars "wasn't waiting for anything in particular. He just liked to look out the window and wait.... Waiting to see what would happen next."

Yes, both Menchin and Henkes have. The former demonstrates the comedy side of Beckett while the latter focuses on the philosophical aspect of it.

8. Why did Beckett, an Irish Protestant whose native language was English, originally write the play in French? What does the French title EN ATTENDANT GODOT best translate as? How did French audiences react to the play?

While Google translates it as "Waiting for Godot," I read it as "In Attendance with Godot" and that, in my opinion, is the more proper title of the play. They are waiting for god while he is actually present. I'm not sure what the French thought of it, but if it's anything like my reaction, they were probably confused and not that happy.

9. Why was the American premiere of WAITING FOR GODOT in a city in Florida rather than on a Broadway stage in New York City? What was

the critical reception and what was the audience response to that first American performance?

Because of how long and sporadic the play is, I doubt anyone reading it the first time would like it because they simply wouldn't understand it. Such a confusing play would never be premiered on Broadway. The critical reception was likely that it mixed comedy and tragedy, which wasn't very appealing, and thus the response to the first American performance was probably largely negative.

10. If I've read or seen Harold Pinter's 1960 play THE DUMB WAITER (as all of us have) or Tom Stoppard's 1967 play ROSENCRANTZ AND GUILDENSTERN ARE DEAD (as several of us have) how, specifically, will it be clear to me that both these playwrights not only admired Samuel Beckett's new approach to theater but were influenced, in particular, by his 1952 play WAITING FOR GODOT?

I don't know about the Stoppard play, but "The Dumb Waiter" is definitely influenced by "Waiting for Godot." As a matter of fact, the dialogue is so similar that we could practically replace Estragon with Gus and Vladimir with Ben (though Gus is a bit extreme with his stupidity-comedy, and Ben is extreme with his harshness).

11. How good or bad is Mr. Eidelberg's timing in "teaching" WAITING FOR GODOT during the 2020 coronavirus pandemic? (When Mr. Eidelberg first taught WAITING FOR GODOT to 12th-graders back in the late 1980's, a young lady who was born in Vietnam in the mid-1960's and went on to be her graduating class's valedictorian, complained to him that he should never have taught such a depressing play to young high school students.)

The timing is very good. Most people have nothing to do during the pandemic besides school, and so they wait for it to end just as Estragon and Vladimir wait for Godot. For a valedictorian, she's a bit pessimistic, and I would assume would advise strongly against teaching it during the pandemic.

12. If it is true (and it is) that Beckett considered his 1950's play WAITING FOR GODOT to be a tragi-comedy (very much unlike Eugene O'Neill's 1946 dark and nihilistic play THE ICEMAN COMETH), can WAITING FOR GODOT still be considered a tragi-comedy in today's world?

96

Personally, I dislike the tragic aspect of Beckett's play, especially the suicide parts. The comedy is okay but the tragic aspect is too heavy and dampens the comical side of it. In today's world, or any time period, it should be considered tragi-comedy because it has elements of both, but I wouldn't consider it one of the best tragi-comedies.

13. The play's absurd, right?

Yes, a bit too much for my liking.

Gamal is an upper junior who lives on Staten Island and commutes to Hunter College by ferry, bus, and subway. Gamal is majoring in history and adolescent education, minoring in political science, and wants to be a secondary school social studies teacher. On Day 1 of our class, Gamal indicated that I looked very familiar to him but he knew he had never taken a course with me before (my only other course at Hunter is on "The Teacher and Student in Literature").

It turned out that I recognized him, too, as a fellow student in a Hunter College history class I had taken as a senior citizen auditor about a year before in which Gamal was enrolled for credit as a history major. When that connection clicked for the two of us, Gamal said something like, "Oh yes, I remember you, you were that older guy who liked to talk in class a lot, just like me."

Gamal wound up requesting that an Incomplete be entered by me on May 11 as his tentative course grade for "The Literature of Waiting" since he had decided to self-quarantine after members of his family were hit by the coronavirus. Gamal felt that now that he was in what he termed the "coronavirus anxiety category," a reasonable time extension for the work he was missing would enable him to complete the course to both his and my satisfaction. Before the month of May was over, the talkative older guy was able to change Gamal's Incomplete to a complete "A."

Portrait of On-Campus and Distance-Learner Gamal

March 12 / Dear Professor,

This is Gamal from ENGL 25146 on Tuesdays and Thursdays from 5:30 to 6:50 PM. I will not be here today due to being sick. I've actually been a little sick since Tuesday and still feel well enough to attend class, but the CUNY Chancellor sent out an email and is now telling all students who are sick to not attend classes. So I will be out today due to the heightened state of alert.

As for assignments, would you like me to email you?

I will be here next Tuesday.

Sincerely,

Gamal

March 15 / Professor Eidelberg,

You stated to hand in last Thursday's assignments "by this weekend," so here they are on Sunday 3/15. It's just that the last few days have been a blur and I am still in a state of confusion.

Attached is my CW/HW assignment for the piece of creative writing inspired by the personal waiting journal. I have also attached answers to the two out of four questions you asked.

Speaking of the former, I believe that I handed that assignment in to you at our last physical session, but attached it again just in case.

Sincerely,

Gamal

March 17 / Hello, Colleagues,

A brief but really important message: if you currently do not have the email address of each and every other member of your independent reading group, please email me right away to get those email addresses you are missing.

In the next three weeks, not only will everyone in a group (and that's everyone!) be in direct contact with all their other group members as part of a soon-to-be-announced newly devised way for "oral communication" to again be a part of your independent reading assignment but also at least one other activity in our coursework before the end of the semester will require all group members to be in regular email contact and, perhaps, telephone/cellphone contact, with one another.

Start to think of your 5-person group as a mini-off-campus class in "The Literature of Waiting" – one that I will also be involved in. Details to follow on the next several Blackboard announcements, so don't delay getting from me any contact information you are missing.

Collegially,

Bob Eidelberg

March 17 / Dear Professor Eidelberg,

I do NOT have the email address of each and every member of my independent reading group.

Sincerely,

Gamal

March 18 / Thank you, Professor,

The emails for Wardah (Malik) and Fawzi are not accurate.

Best,

Gamal

March 26 / Dear Professor Eidelberg,

This is Gamal from Waiting. I would like to request an extension of one day for all that is due today. The reason is due to a personal matter. I could go more into detail if you wish.

Sincerely,

Gamal

March 30 / Hello, Colleagues,

I am writing to request that you send on a pdf attachment (for serious consideration in our course's book SOME DAY) the first-rate piece of creative writing that you did in connection with our study of WAITING FOR LEFTY by Clifford Odets (revised vignette, changed vignette, new vignette). Your CW/HW piece MUST be accessible from a clickable pdf icon on your covering email – and I really need to have it before the end of this week if you can.

In any case, please also acknowledge getting this email from me as soon as you read it.

Many thanks.

Collegially,

Bob Eidelberg

March 30 / From Gamal

Will do; I acknowledge.

March 31 / Dear Professor Eidelberg,

Attached are the submissions for Session #17 and Session #18 on "Waiting for the Barbarians." I feel like I owe an explanation for submitting Session #17 late. Although I've previously sent you an email highlighting reasons why I will be submitting it late, I only stated that I will submit it late by one day, not during the next lesson.

The reason is because these past few weeks a lot has happened and I haven't been able to focus. To give an example, I had to purchase a laptop in order to be able to do assignments, since before then I only relied on the computers at Hunter College to do so. So that was one hindrance to my schoolwork. I also had to apply to emergency aid, get food for the family, make arrangements for my two jobs, etc. Lastly, my brother is currently in self-quarantine and I'm currently debating whether or not to get tested.

With that said, I said I would submit it only one day late, but clearly I was wrong, so I do apologize.

Sincerely,

Gamal

April 2 / Dear Professor,

Attached are today's works. I've also emailed my group the essay on "Robinson Crusoe" as requested.

Sincerely,

Gamal

April 4 / Dear Professor Eidelberg,

I've always wondered how people in the past lived, and I guess I shouldn't "wait" before asking. I'm wondering if I can ask three questions from way back.

1. *Have you ever met someone who lived in the 1800s? How was that like? Ever met someone who lived through the Civil War as a child?*
2. *You were an adult when JFK was tragically assassinated, can you share your thoughts on your experiences and the gravity of such an event?*
3. *Have you ever lived on a Kibbutz or any other commune?*

Best,

Gamal

April 4 / Hello, Gamal,

I'm old but I'm not that old (actually I guess I am!), so "no" to Questions 1 and 3 (except that my maternal grandmother was born in 1890 in Austria and gave birth to my mother in 1920 in Brooklyn, New York).

Wait for it: as for Question 2, I was in my very early 20's and, coincidentally, had just moved back to New York City from Houston, Texas, when President Kennedy was assassinated in Dallas (which I had never even visited) when I was working (fresh out of grad school) as a general assignment reporter and second-string arts critic for the Houston Chronicle newspaper.

I was in my parents' Brooklyn house — in my old bedroom — when, Arnold, a high school friend of mine called to tell me that he had just heard on the news that the president had been shot. I actually took the call sitting on the edge of my boyhood bed. I was in disbelief and shock (my first American assassination outside of the history books I had read) since for someone of my age and politics, Kennedy was a true hero – and I think his death, in retrospect, changed the course of American and world history (for the worse).

Collegially,

Bob Eidelberg

April 4 / From Gamal

Thank you for the story, Professor.

The reason I asked is because I figured that there was not an event in modern American history more shocking or powerful as President Kennedy's assassination.

Thanks for your first-hand account, and quite an interesting backstory you've got. It is one of those moments that everyone remembers what they were doing.

The reason I asked is because I always wondered what it's like to live during a historical event, and now as a result of this pandemic, I'm finding out that it ain't pretty to be the protagonists in history books.

By the way, here's a One More Thing.

It is a haiku I made inspired by my morning.

You know what's scary?
Not ambulances wailing.
But the birds' chirping.

Here's another haiku related to waiting out this pandemic.

Hiding and masking.
We are living in a cave.
Secluded. Waiting.

April 4 / Hello, Colleagues,

Please read carefully; print, sign, and date at the bottom (so that your written work in this course can legally be published by me on your behalf); and mail back to me at my home address as soon as you can.

CONSENT FORM

On this date I fully agree to permit Mr. Robert Eidelberg of the Hunter College English Department to include without qualification in the book he is arranging to self-publish (with the working title SOME DAY: A CREATIVE WRITING COURSE, WITH TIME ON ITS HANDS, HAS ITS SAY ON "THE LITERATURE OF WAITING") any of the pieces of academic and creative writing or any illustrative drawings I have produced for Mr. Eidelberg's English 25146 class during the spring 2020 semester, whether done in class or at home. I understand, further, that I will receive no financial compensation or other consideration for my contributions to this book other than that I will be listed as the author for each written piece or sketch of mine that is actually used and that I will also be named on a separate page as one of the "college collaborators" to our course's book, SOME DAY.

Your legal full name printed neatly: _____

Your signature: _____Today's date: _____

April 5 / Dear Professor Eidelberg,

I do not have access to a printer at home; is it possible to write it out and mail it to you?

Best,

Gamal

April 7 / From Gamal to groupmate Fawzi (as well as to Professor Eidelberg, as required),

I am wondering, Fawzi, if you can elaborate when you stated about the novel "Robinson Crusoe": "I don't think the waiting is realistic." Is this perhaps because you feel like the protagonist lost hope and gave up searching? With that in mind, is it possible to wait and be hopeless at the same time? I feel like when it comes to waiting, there has to be a little bit of hope involved in the process. I can't personally visualize hopeless waiting.

Best,

Gamal

April 8 / Hello, Gamal, from Professor Eidelberg,

How would you characterize "despair" if not as "hopeless waiting"?

Collegially,

Bob Eidelberg

April 8 / Hi Professor,

Despair is indeed the absence of hope; however, when it comes to waiting, when one is in despair they are left with two options – they can accept their fate and no longer wait or they can become intrinsically motivated out of lack of options. It is like cornering an animal, the only option left is to fight or be eaten. There is no waiting in fighting, rather the entire focus is on the present situation. Waiting, on the other hand, it's thinking of a future outcome.

Best,

Gamal

April 11 / Dear Professors,

If you are receiving this email then that means I am in one of your classes.

My brother has indeed caught the coronavirus and is currently quarantining. I have been in physical contact with him recently and I've been developing symptoms over the past week.

As a result, I am currently self-quarantining as well. I've already contacted the New York State COVID-19 Hotline to arrange getting tested, hopefully they don't refuse testing me, they'll get back to me later this week.

Please do not worry, I am feeling okay. It's worse in the early morning and at night.

What does this mean in terms of schoolwork? At the moment, not much. I will still continue to hand in assignments that are due (and late assignments that I am missing).

I'll keep you updated. Stay safe.

Sincerely,

Gamal

PS: Here is the number for the NYS COVID-19 Hotline if you need it: (888) 364-3065

April 11 / From Professor Eidelberg,

Hang in there, Gamal. My thoughts are with you and your family.

Collegially,

Bob Eidelberg

April 28 / Dear Professors,

This is Gamal from one of your classes. I want to give an update on the email I sent 2 weeks previously.

After 3+ weeks of symptoms, I have now tested "Not Detected," i.e., negative for COVID-19.

I have been feeling much better lately, and I am currently rushing to get back on track for all my schoolwork. I apologize if I was late for any assignments due, I'm currently working to get all my past assignments in ASAP. I also want to thank you all for your support and for reaching out to me.

Oh, and my brother, sister-in-law, and other family members are doing well too and recovering.

Once again, thank you, and I hope the rest of the semester goes well for all.

Sincerely,

Gamal

April 28 / Dear Professor Eidelberg,

I am definitely in the coronavirus anxiety category, and want to personally apologize for missing work these past three weeks.

I have done no work for any of my classes and this past week has been a nightmare for me trying to catch up. I promise to make up all the work needed.

Sincerely,

Gamal

April 28 / Dear Professor,

Attached is the "Some Day" Consent Form. I took a picture of it. From my understanding, you either want us to take a picture of it OR mail it to you? Or do you want us to take a picture of it AND mail it to you?

Sincerely,

Gamal

April 29 / Hello, Gamal,

Thanks, especially, for this most recent of your several emails to me. I feel your anxiety and predicament, so let me run some possibilities by you based on our shared desire for you to do quality work without undue stress but also based on my curiosity as to what kind of final course grade you want to be working toward (since the Gamal I remember seemed to be aiming for an A or A+, but that might not be the Gamal recovering from the coronavirus, who is, as you point out, behind in all his classes and not just his favorite one – smiles!).

So, one possibility is to let me give you an Incomplete on May 11 when I enter final grades and give you until June 1 to either make up all your missed assignments since Session #19 (by checking my Blackboard announcements for Sessions from #20 on through 28) or a combination of some of those missed assignments plus some replacement work assignments (there are like 14 of them listed across two or three Blackboard announcements).

Another possibility is to do as much quality current and replacement work as you can from now until the May 7 last "session" of the course with however much stress you can bear and still do that quantity of quality work to earn a B+ or A- (or, conceivably an "A" but not an "A+").

Or, well, you tell me, now that I've given you something to think about. But the key factors here are: amount of work time allotted, nature of the work done, quality of the work done, quantity of the work done, competition from your other courses, critical need to minimize your overall stress, and the letter grade you realistically think you can qualify for.

Collegially,

Bob Eidelberg

May 3 / From Gamal,

Thank you for the timely response. I have taken some time to think about it. I think an INC grade would be better for now, and then I finish the assignments by June 1.

PS: How does an INC grade work? Does it change to a letter grade once complete?

Sincerely,

Gamal

May 9 / Hello, Colleagues,

According to my records, I have not yet received your signed consent form for your work to be published (other than anonymously) in our course's book SOME DAY.

As I am about to enter final course grades (including "Incomplete" for several of you) this coming week, I cannot do so (or honor our "Incomplete" agreement) until I have received your consent form. Check a fairly recent Blackboard announcement for a reprint of the form and a reminder of a variety of different ways you can easily send the signed form to me within the next few days.

Please do not delay doing this any longer – and thank you.

Collegially,

Bob Eidelberg

May 9 / Dear Professor,

I already emailed you the consent form several weeks ago, and you replied confirming you received it.

Is there a step I am missing?

Sincerely,

Gamal

May 9 / From Professor Eidelberg,

Oops, you're right. (Not a test; my mistake.)

How are things going?

Collegially,

Bob Eidelberg

May 9 / From Gamal,

Oh okay, sounds good. Phew!

I'm doing well, catching up.

Best,

Gamal

May 9 / Dear Professor,

I am trying to email you all of the coursework that was due but the system is not allowing me to send them because they are being marked as spam.

Do you have another email that I can send my coursework to?

Sincerely,

Gamal

May 21 / Dear Professor Eidelberg,

Attached are all of my assignments in pdf format for ENGL 25146: The Literature of Waiting. Please do let me know if I missed any assignments.

I would like to thank you for giving me the flexibility in completing the assignments for this class. I hope I am not exaggerating when I say I was completely swamped with work for all my classes and could not "wait" to complete them so I can focus my creative energy towards this class.

Hopefully, the quality is up to par compared to pre-pandemic work. I am waiting to return to Hunter in the fall semester (fingers crossed) and continue my academic journey.

One thing I will take away from this class is the following: literature is multifaceted and is human thoughts being put into ink, and when we condense it and look at it through different lenses, such as the concept of waiting, we are able to study how such a specific theme is relevant through not just the text but life in general.

Thank you, Professor.

Sincerely,

Gamal

Massiel is an upper sophomore who lives in the Bronx and commutes to Hunter College by subway. She is majoring in computer science and minoring in history and might go into computer programming as her career.

Massiel was a relatively quiet student during our on-campus classes during the first seven weeks of the term, and she adapted well to distance learning with its emphasis on analytical writing over oral argument. Massiel's diligence, her thoroughness, and her proven academic excellence during both halves of the course earned her an on-time final letter grade of "A."

Portrait of On-Campus and Distance-Learner Massiel

March 12 / Hello,

I've attached the creative writing CW/HW inspired by a journal entry and a written answer to two out of the four questions asked on Blackboard. For further assignments, do you prefer it written out in the body of an email or in an attachment?

Thank you,

Massiel

March 12 / Thanks, Massiel,

Let's keep them, for now, in the body of the email the way you did here. By the way, since we will not be able to meet in groups on campus, you can switch to THE AGE OF INNOCENCE from GREAT EXPECTATIONS for your independent reading if you would like to.

Collegially,

Bob Eidelberg

March 15 / Hello,

In regards to changing groups, I would rather stay with "Great Expectations." I already ordered the book, and am excited to read it. Also, in response to your Blackboard post I do not have the contact information of any colleague. I don't have any specific requests.

Hope all is well,

Massiel

April 2 / Hello,

I've attached my work on "Great Expectations."

Thank you,

Massiel

April 14 / To Massiel from groupmate Nattapat Karmniyanont,

I really enjoyed what you had to say about *"Great Expectations."* I particularly like what you said about Pip having to "wait to see the validity of his expectations" and how we can only realize our mistakes when a lot of our time is long past us. In concurrence with your position, I also believe that *"Great Expectations"* should be included for future semesters of this course for many of the same reasons as you. And although we picked different novels to replace, I can see why you would want to replace *Waiting.* I really like how you talked about waiting in *Waiting for Barbarians* being explored in a larger framework and warrant to be included.

April 14 / Hello,

I hope this email finds you in good health. I have attached my work. I was wondering what is the proper way to send my journal entries. Should I send them each individually or in one big document?

Thank you,

Massiel

April 15 / Hello, Massiel,

There is no need to send all of the journal entries — just the one that inspired the piece of creative writing you are also sending on to me — and those two items can be sent together.

Not so incidentally, excellent work on the four WIZARD OF OZ questions you responded to.

Collegially,

Bob Eidelberg

April 15 / Hello, again, Massiel,

Are you thinking of doing the extra credit CW/HW on a possible fourth character to go with Dorothy on her journey along the yellow brick road in THE WIZARD OF OZ? The flying monkeys have real potential!

Collegially,

Bob Eidelberg

May 7 / Hello, Professor,

I hope all is well. I have attached my final assignment and my extra credit assignment. Also, thank you! I have truly enjoyed and learned so much from your class. I can't help but notice the different forms of waiting in life and art, and how at the end they all amount to a bigger type of waiting.

Massiel

Bianca is a graduating senior living in the Bronx who commutes to Hunter College by subway; she is majoring in sociology and hopes to become a case manager. Bianca found the class intimidating at first, according to another student who spoke to me out of concern for her, and this was later confirmed to me by Bianca herself. Intimidating? Me?

Well, yes, but largely because of my repeated reminders to the class of the course's far-from-traditional credit emphasis on oral participation (55 percent of the final grade). Apparently unaccustomed in her years at Hunter to being so strongly encouraged (pressured?) to speak regularly in class, Bianca, by the mid-point in the course, made a point of letting me know that a trick I had taught her to overcome her shyness was working. (I should add here, and so I will, that my not-everyone's-cup-of-tea sense of humor might also have played a role in Bianca's earlier "distancing" from me and her fellow students.)

When it came to thoughtout insights and a good imagination, Bianca's academic and creative writing was frequently impressive and I thought to myself that she was going to come more into her own during distance learning; instead, Bianca became a victim of what she herself termed these "worrisome times."

Portrait of On-Campus Bianca

February 29 / Hello Professor,

I would like a copy of "The Dumb Waiter" that Valeria scanned. Thank you in advance.

Kind regards,

Bianca

Portrait of Distance-Learner Bianca

March 25 / Hello Selected Colleagues,

I hope you are physically and psychologically well during these stressful times since March 10, but I have noticed that since the start of distant learning you have not been fully involved in the work of our course as detailed in the Calendar of Sessions that you have in your possession (for Sessions #14 through #18, in particular) as well as in the changes, additions, and subtractions to the required reading and writing listed under those sections as detailed in six Blackboard announcements posted by me on a regular basis.

Besides from the fact that all CUINY faculty are now being asked to report the names of such students to, in your cases, Hunter College, I would like to reach out to you once again before I do anything in an official capacity that might jeopardize your status at Hunter. (Not so incidentally, I have sent personal email requests to several of you for pdf attachments of your first-rate pieces of creative writing done while we all were meeting together as a class on campus and those emails were neither complied with nor acknowledged.)

Seriously, I do hope you are reasonably okay, but I would feel a lot better if I knew that directly from you.

I hope you will respond to this email within the next day or so.

Collegially,

Bob Eidelberg

March 25 / Hello Professor,

I sent the "Waiting for the Barbarians" assignment prior to the due date. I'm assuming you haven't received it since I was sent this email for limited involvement/non-involvement.

I'm all right health-wise. I hope you're also doing well during these worrisome times.

Kind regards,

Bianca

April 3 / Hello everyone (in the independent reading group for the novel ELEANOR OLIPHANT IS COMPLETELY FINE),

I hope you guys are doing well and trying to keep your spirits up during these scary and troublesome times. I've attached my essay arguing for the novel to be included in the course alongside "Waiting" and "Waiting for the Barbarians."

Kind regards,

Bianca

May 11 / Hello Professor,

I've attached a photo of my signed, handwritten version of the consent form for our course's book SOME DAY. I would like to receive an INC so I can complete the course work I'm missing before the end of summer.

I hope you're healthy and doing well.

Kind regards,

Bianca

Note from the Instructor:

In response to Bianca's request to have till the end of August to complete the work assigned for Sessions 17 - 28, Mr. Eidelberg said that it would be best for Bianca to work toward completing as much work as possible by June 1, at which point he would change the Incomplete to a passing letter grade. Bianca did do satisfactorily all of the written work involved in Session 19's individual reading and writing and its group sharing study of the novel ELEANOR OLIPHANT IS COMPLETELY FINE, and Mr. Eidelberg ultimately entered a B+ passing grade for Bianca to supersede the INC.

May 29 / Hello Professor,

I've realized that I received a B+ instead of an INC and upon reading your prior emails, I'm assuming this is the result of my not sending any assignments after our correspondence. I understand, and would therefore like to opt out of receiving a letter grade and instead get CR. Thank you in advance.

Kind regards,

Bianca

Andrea (pronounced with the greater stress on the middle syllable) is an upper junior who lives in Queens, works long hours in a pharmacy (of all places during the pandemic!), and is majoring in biology in hopes of becoming a doctor "practicing medicine."

Andrea was running an "A-" at the mid-point of the semester but opted for a temporary Incomplete grade for the course (through the end of May, but later extended to the end of June) in order to give herself time and space to make up all her missing work, which dated from about a week before the course went into distance learning (Session #17) through the last session of the course, #28, on May 7. How that worked out – the narrative arc is something I know Andrea herself would appreciate – may have had something to do with the fine art of emailing. Or not.

Portrait of On-Campus and Distance-Learner Andrea

March 10 (ironically, the last time we all met as an on-campus class) / Hi Professor,

I am so sorry I wasn't able to make it to class today, I have been working since Friday, and my body shut down today, also I have been sneezing and coughing due to hopefully seasonal allergies. However, I will send you today's assignments later on and hopefully, if I am feeling better, I will see you on Thursday ... I can't wait!

Andrea

March 10 / Hello, Andrea,

I'll look for the assignments "later on" – and I'll look for a newly revitalized Andrea in class on Thursday the 12th.

Collegially,

Bob Eidelberg

March 10 / Hi Professor,

These are three of the four that I owe you. Will send the fourth to you as soon as possible.

March 22 / Hello, Andrea,

If you have a fairly correctly typed and unmarked copy of your early February letter to a friend that you were reconnecting with (based on a "some day" song of your choice), could you email it to me at our course's email – within the next few days – for possible use in our course's book SOME DAY?

Many thanks.

Collegially,

Bob Eidelberg

March 25 / From Andrea

I am sharing a file with you – the song "Somewhere" from "West Side Story."

March 30 / Hi Professor,

I was looking over the assignments for our selected group-reading of "The Age of Innocence" and realized I had probably sent the email asking for my colleagues' emails to your Hunter College faculty email, which I had forgotten you don't check, instead of to our course's email. I am very sorry to not have realized this sooner. Is there a way you can send me their emails, so I can get in touch with them as soon as possible?

Thank you,

Andrea

May 12 / Hello, Colleagues,

This is the third notice I've sent out to you and until I get the required consent form within the week, I will not be able to enter a letter grade or an Incomplete for you for our course this term.

According to my records, I have not yet received your signed consent form for your work to be published (other than anonymously) in our course's book SOME DAY.

As I am about to enter final course grades (including "Incomplete" for several of you) this coming week, I cannot do so (or honor our "Incomplete" agreement) until I have received your consent form. Check a fairly recent Blackboard announcement for a reprint of the form and a reminder of a variety of different ways you can easily send the signed form to me within the next few days.

Please do not delay doing this any longer – and thank you.

Collegially,

Bob Eidelberg

May 19 / Hello Professor!,

I have sent on my signed consent form and I am working on getting in the assignments to you by this week. Concentration has not been easy at all. However, you will receive the ten journal entries by later today or tomorrow morning and the rest of the assignments soon after. Thank you so much for the patience.

Andrea

June 7 / Hello Professor,

I hope all is well. I'm emailing you because I never got a response on the assignments. Perhaps I didn't email them or sent them somewhere else. I want to know if I still have an opportunity to send them to you or some other thing that I can do to save my grade. Please let me know. I am so sorry to inconvenience you like this.

Looking forward to hearing from you,

Andrea

June 7 / Hello, Andrea,

I'm glad to hear from you at last and see from this email that you must be reasonably well.

However, I must tell you in all sincerity that the most puzzling thing about this email, Andrea, is the sentence "Perhaps I didn't send them or sent them somewhere else" as the likely explanation for your not getting any response from me on the assignments.

I have not heard from you for ages, not even the collegial courtesy of a response to my several emails to you urgently reminding you that you had only to June 1 to send me sufficient quality work to change the Incomplete grade entered on May 11 to a passing letter grade.

So, since my records show that I have absolutely none of the multiple assignments for any of the sessions from Session #17 through Session # 28 (in other words, no work since even before we went onto distance learning), my question of you is: what do you propose to do about any of this since, as of the end of this month, I am not a teacher of record at Hunter College and don't know if I will be when the fall term begins at the very end of August?

And is there in your mind an actual passing non-Incomplete grade that you have plans "to save"?

Collegially,

Bob Eidelberg

Monday, June 8 (at 12:21 am) / From Andrea,

I truly apologize for this.

Monday, June 8 (at 12:24 am) / From Andrea,

I indeed apologize. These weeks and months have been very difficult for me and I have indeed been pushing to finish all the assignments. If there is a chance for me to resend my work I will absolutely and gladly accept it; if not I might have to make the course a no-credit course due to my lack of communication.

Monday, June 8 / Hello, Andrea,

I accept your apologies. Naturally, I'm sorry for the difficulties you've been having and will look in my email inbox today and tomorrow (but in all fairness to you and to our other formerly Incomplete colleagues, not thereafter) for all the homework and replacement assignments you have already completed. Based on how many there are and their overall quality, I'll get back to you by no later than Thursday as to what courses of action might be available to you. (By the way, are you in a better or worse situation with your other courses?)

Collegially,

Bob Eidelberg

June 9 / Hello, Andrea,

Thank you for the 14 pieces of missing and replacement work I received in our course's email inbox early today, and which I immediately read over and evaluated.

In fairness to several other Incomplete students, who submitted equivalent quality work by the June 1 deadline (including quality work on books that you apparently did not read, like THE WIZARD OF OZ, THE DECAMERON, EINSTEIN'S DREAMS, and most importantly, WAITING FOR GODOT), I can give you at most a grade of B or B+ at this time.

Does that work for you, or do you want to go for an A- by submitting additional work over the next week or so at most on the novels you did not deal with?

Please let me know as soon as today.

Collegially,

Bob Eidelberg

June 9 / From Andrea,

I'd love that chance. I'll get back to you in the next couple of days. Thank you so much.

June 18 / Hello to the Four English 25146 "Incomplete" Colleagues Who Have Until June 30 to Submit Their Missing Homework Assignments and Replacement Work,

I hope you four are relatively well and working on your assignments relatively diligently.

As I've mentioned previously, on the first of July I must officially contact Hunter College and inform them of which letter grade your Incomplete is to be changed to. Since I have not received much work from some of you in recent weeks (despite my stressing the importance of your sending me each piece as you complete it so that I have time to read it carefully and evaluate it fairly), I am concerned that I will be inundated with lots of writing from the four of you in the last three days of June.

Here's how I feel about that: with so little time for me to read and evaluate that much work, it is highly unlikely that any of you would wind up with a mark of A- or A. If that is not an actual concern for you, I would have no problem entering a mark of either B or B+ (depending) for you on next Monday, June 22, based on my record of all that you have done and done well both in our thirteen on-campus classes and since distance learning began after March 10. If that works for you, please let me know right away.

And if you still want the time until June 30 to work at home some more to get a final course grade of A- or A, then you MUST send me something substantial that you have recently written for the course by that same date — next Monday, June 22.

If you have any questions about any of this, of course email them to me immediately.

Collegially,

Bob Eidelberg

June 29 / From Andrea,

These are the responses to "Waiting for Godot" that you've been waiting for. The past several weeks have been a rollercoaster, and I did not think they would affect me in the way that they did – but thank you so much, Professor, for the numerous opportunities to make up the work and for your "timely" reminders.

Andrea

July 1 / Hello, Andrea,

Just wanted to let you know that based on your meeting our July 1 deadline with a sufficient number of quality pieces of written work (made-up missing assignments, replacement assignments, extra-credit pieces), I have formally requested Hunter College to change your Incomplete to a final letter grade of "A-" in The Literature of Waiting course.

Congratulations on what was a far from easy or easily assumed academic achievement in these troubled times. Have a stress-free, healthy, and happy summer!

Collegially,

Bob Eidelberg

July 2 / From Andrea,

I am truly grateful, and I apologize for not completely showing my full potential. I hope you take care of yourself, and hopefully I will see you in Hunter once all the waiting is over. Thank you for a very inspiring semester, and an excellent example of waiting!

Andrea

Ryan, a graduating senior, lives in (or "on") Staten Island and commutes to Hunter College by ferry, bus, and subway. Majoring in creative writing (with a minor in art history), Ryan considers himself a first-rate writer (which, it turns out, he is). Boyfriend of Maxine, the two of them enter class together every time and sit next to each other in adjoining rows.

Ryan participates in class somewhat less than Maxine but is super attentive. Ryan and Maxine were the very last students in the class that I saw just before the campus got closed for the pandemic – they were together outside Hunter West in the rain when I was headed home the night of March 10 and we acknowledged each other's presence and said a last "goodnight." Ryan got an on-time "A" as his final grade in "The Literature of Waiting" course.

Portrait of On-Campus and Distance-Learner Ryan

March 17 / Hello, Colleagues,

A brief but really important message: if you currently do not have the email address of each and every other member of your independent reading group, please email me right away to get those email addresses you are missing.

In the next three weeks, not only will everyone in a group (and that's everyone!) be in direct contact with all their other group members as part of a soon-to-be-announced newly devised way for "oral communication" to again be a part of your independent reading assignment but also at least one other activity in our coursework before the end of the semester will require all group members to be in regular email contact and, perhaps, telephone/cellphone contact, with one another.

Start to think of your 5-person group as a mini-off-campus class in THE LITERATURE OF WAITING – one that I will also be involved in. Details to follow on the next several Blackboard announcements, so don't delay getting from me any contact information you are missing.

Collegially,

Bob Eidelberg

March 17 / Hi Professor,

Could you please send me the emails of the people in my group? I'm not sure exactly who is in the group – I'm in Cape May at present, where there are no cases, and I don't have all my papers with me.

Thanks in advance and hope you're staying healthy!

Ryan

March 23 / Hello, Colleagues,

If you have a fairly correctly typed and unmarked copy of your early February letter to a friend that you were reconnecting with (based on a "some day" song of your choice), could you email it to me at our course's email — within the next few days – for possible use in our course's book SOME DAY?

Collegially,

Bob Eidelberg

March 23 / Hi Professor,

Please find my letter attached.

Best,

Ryan

March 24 / One more thing, Professor:

Since we're in quarantine, Maxine and I ordered a game called Cards Against Humanity – do you know it? – and in perusing the instruction manual, which was outrageously funny and clever, I came across a section of rules (rules that, have you a sense of sarcasm?, are not to be taken seriously). One of these rules is written as follows:

Wait for Godot

"At the start of the game, instead of drawing a hand, players stare at the pile of white cards. After an indeterminate length of time, players move their gaze to the pile of black cards. The game doesn't begin. How can it begin? It has already ended. In the gloom, players shift their cloudy gaze from pile to pile. Is it a trick of the light, or do the black cards and the white cards seem to converge in an indistinguishable grayness? Mote by mote, dust settles on the cards. Nobody accumulates points. Nobody wins."

We thought this was hilarious. Hope you think so too!

Best,

Ryan

PS - is "apollo" or "glamor" our course email?

March 24 / Hello, Colleagues,

I am making a second request for a particular CW/HW because I fear (since I got only one response from the 16 of you) that it did not reach most of you. So, please send me (or send me again!) a pdf copy (it has to be a pdf, sorry!) attached to an email on the "How to Be a Waiter" CW/ HW you did earlier in the semester.

Collegially,

Bob Eidelberg

March 24 / Hi Professor,

You've so far asked me to submit two – not sure if you only meant one, or meant two, or meant neither, or if I sent to the wrong email, or if it's all been lost to the ether and is drifting in an infinite void – regardless, here are the two pieces I think you want from me.

All the best,

Ryan

March 25 / Hello Ryan (and by extension just a few feet away, Maxine),

As I do have a sense of sarcasm — and no shame — many thanks for the "Wait for Godot." It would have been perfect if you could have shared it in class on campus during a close (not-distant!) learning experience in Room HW404. But then, if not for your quarantine, you would not have known about it. Or maybe you would have. Only Godot knows — and he's not talking ('cause he's not coming).

Answers to Questions:

(1) the "apollo" is my personal email which I've been slipping into during distant teaching (irony of situation?); "glamor" remains our course email, of course;

(2) of course I thought it was hilarious (though I don't know the game, but will now look into it, so thanks); you wouldn't have told me about it if you weren't confident about my reaction.

Collegially,

Bob Eidelberg

March 25 / Good morning Professor,

Glad you got a kick out of It!

I've attached the two pdfs here – I was under the impression that I had done that in my gmail. Let me know if this works out better.

Best,

Ryan

April 2 / Hi Professor,

Here are the pieces you have asked for. I do not presently have the "Telephone Call" writing at my disposal, but I can maybe get it to you this weekend.

Best,

Ryan

April 24 / Howdy folks in our group on ROSENCRANTZ AND GUILDENSTERN ARE DEAD,

Hope you're all well. Here's a song by Bruce Springsteen called Growin' Up. Who doesn't love The Boss? Also, what better song could be chosen on the subject of growin' up than one called Growin' Up? This is one of my dad's favorite songs, and I heard it on one of the benefit call-in TV concert things for pandemic relief, so I figured enough elements of fate had come together to send this one through.

Take care everyone, be well,

Ryan

May 3 / Hi Professor,

I hope you are well and not, as I am, slowly losing your mind in the midst of this thing. I have a question as regards the consent form – I'm not sure it will reach you by mail at the necessary date, and I do not presently have access to a printer/scanner to get the form to you electronically. Is there a way I can write it out and send you a picture attachment? Or could an email version suffice? I'd hate to miss out on this.

Let me know and be well!

Thanks,

Ryan

May 4 / Hello, Ryan (and Maxine, too, if that's okay),

Good to hear from you, Ryan — it's been a while.

Sorry you're slowly losing that creative mind of yours (slowly is worse than quickly, right?) but I actually thought the many creative writing assignments from me these past four weeks were going to help you through (as well as produce more good stuff for our course's book SOME DAY).

Any chance of your doing the three from THE WIZARD OF OZ, EINSTEIN'S DREAMS, and WAITING FOR GODOT (or any of the 12 or so up-your-alley creative replacement activities detailed on my Blackboard announcements in recent weeks) by Monday, May 11, when I enter final letter-grade course marks? (Same enticement to Maxine — you hear me, Maxine? — whose distance learning homework record is a bit better than Ryan's.)

Both of you were achieving a solid A- when the course went under house arrest on March 12, and I don't want to be presumptions about what kind of final grade in the course you need to or want to get as graduating seniors, but you might want to drop me a hint (or not — no pressure).

As to the consent form, I guess you missed the recent detailed announcement in Blackboard that gave several alternative ways of getting the required form to me, but you seem to have figured out on your own a couple that I mentioned, so go for it (encourage Maxine, if you can, to do likewise).

Collegially,

Bob Eidelberg

May 4 / Hi Professor,

Thank you for your concern, and I apologize for my absence in the recent sessions. This whole situation has created a lot of new familial responsibilities for me that have to do with income and caretaking, and on the whole have just derailed my schoolwork, not just in this class but in all of them. I should've reached out – I know how understanding you've been with other students, but days keep getting away from me and I keep finding myself behind.

However! I have the next few days to kick into overdrive and turn in assignments. To answer your question, yes, I do intend to submit the writings associated with The Wizard of Oz and Einstein's Dreams, as I've finished reading them and begun to think about them. I can have those to you by the end of the day. I should be through Waiting for Godot tomorrow, and will send the two assignments then, if that's alright with you. What's more, I definitely could use the extra credit, and several of the options you offered appeal to me, so I will have that for you by Thursday. As for the consent form, I will work that out and send today as well.

Again, I apologize for disappearing. Without the in-person class, which I've always enjoyed, it's very easy to slip and start missing. The online learning just isn't the same. I hope this all works for you – if it's too much at once, or if there is a different way you'd like to go about it, please let me know. And I do very much appreciate your patience in this time – it's the kind of thing that gets people through. I will forward on this info to Maxine as well.

All the best,

Ryan

May 4 / Hi Professor,

Please find homeworks and an image of my written consent attached.

May 7 / Hi Professor,

Please find assignments attached.

Thank you for such a wonderful semester. It's been a real pleasure to work with you and examine all these excellent works of literature, both creatively and analytically. Although we were interrupted mid-semester by this pandemic, I felt connected to the class and still had a great experience. Thank you for everything, and I look forward to seeing our book!

All the best,

Ryan

Maxine is a senior majoring in sociology and minoring in psychology; she is unsure of her career goals. Maxine lives on the West Side of the borough of Manhattan (home to Hunter College on the East side of the borough) and, as I wrote when I introduced the portrait of her fellow classmate and boyfriend, Ryan, during our almost fourteen weeks of on-campus classes, Maxine and Ryan would always enter our classroom together precisely at 5:35 pm every Tuesday and Thursday and proceed to sit down next to each other in adjoining rows. They would likewise leave the room together when our class ended 75 minutes later at 6:50 pm (because my students hate it when I go even a minute over!).

A more active class participant than her collegial companion Ryan, Maxine was one of the few students who almost always handwrote her assignments (no computer?). But Maxine's handwriting was close to illegible (she has admitted as much), and she rarely skipped every other line to give me a fighting chance at deciphering her scrawls (and to provide room for my generally positive comments). I believe that after the shutdown of our campus, Maxine was one of the many students Hunter College gave a free laptop or tablet to for remote writing. I remember that Maxine was particularly interested in being part of the collaborative discussion group that would be reading the contemporary novel ELEANOR OLIPHANT IS COMPLETELY FINE, which deals with the title character's mental problems. Not being "completely fine" during distance learning was also one of the challenges Maxine worked to overcome.

And, oh yes, as I mentioned in connection with Ryan, "the couple" of Maxine and Ryan were the last two of my students that I saw that final night of on-campus teaching and learning: the two of them were standing in the rain outside the Hunter West building as I existed to go home by subway to Brooklyn. We exchanged hellos and goodnights. Maxine eventually earned an on-time "A-" grade in our course on "The Literature of Waiting."

Portrait of On-Campus and Distance-Learner Maxine

March 17 / Hello, Colleagues,

A brief but really important message: if you currently do not have the email address of each and every other member of your independent reading group, please email me right away to get those email addresses you are missing.

In the next three weeks, not only will everyone in a group (and that's everyone!) be in direct contact with all their other group members as part of a soon-to-be-announced newly devised way for "oral communication" to again be a part of your independent reading assignment but also at least one other activity in our coursework before the end of the semester will require all group members to be in regular email contact and, perhaps, telephone/cellphone contact, with one another.

Start to think of your 5-person group as a mini-off-campus class in "The Literature of Waiting" – one that I will also be involved in. Details to follow on the next several Blackboard announcements, so don't delay getting from me any contact information you are missing.

Collegially,

Bob Eidelberg

April 7 / Hi from Maxine (who felt strongly about being allowed to join the group of students reading the novel ELEANOR OLIPHANT IS COMPLETELY FINE) to the "guys" in the ELEANOR OLIPHANT IS COMPLETELY FINE group,

I'll be sending my essay later today or tomorrow. I took a little time off from school to deal with some mental health issues.

Maxine

April 7 (about four hours later) Hi "Completely Fine" guys,

Here's the essay, we're supposed to edit all of them?

Maxine

April 7 / Hello, Maxine, from Professor Eidelberg (who gets copies of all group correspondence)

No, Maxine — and please stay calm, now that you're doing so much better!

You're not to edit any of them; you're to react to one (only one) of the ones written by a groupmate on the same work of lit. Okay?

Then, send — on a pdf — your written reaction to that person AND to me.

Collegially,

Bob Eidelberg

April 14 / Hi from groupmate Anne-Lilja, a lower junior and psychology major, to the four other students in the group reading Gail Honeyman's 2017 novel ELEANOR OLIPHANT IS COMPLETELY FINE,

I hope you're all doing well and staying safe. I apologize for this being so late. I also needed to take some time off for mental health issues, in addition to responsibilities at home. Here's my essay for sharing within the group.

Best,

Anne-Lilja

April 22 / From Maxine,

This is probably my favorite poem to date although I don't do as much poetry reading as Ryan. Although it doesn't exactly embody waiting I think of it that way for two reasons: One, I believe this poem shows what it's like to have been waiting all that time to share your thoughts and experiences with others and to finally have it. Second, this poem shows the two waiting to do all of these things together like go to Barcelona or see pieces at the Frick.

https://poets.org/poem/having-coke-you

Maxine

May 3 / From Mr. Eidelberg: Options You Have for a Passing Course Grade in English 25146 (The Literature of Waiting)

Hello,

It's been a while since I have heard from you either by a response to an email of mine, a Blackboard request, or a significant number of homework assignments turned in (even late), and I am concerned about your physical and mental health and your anxiety status during these worrisome times.

Also, I don't know whether you are doing any of the currently required reading in our "Literature of Waiting" course and are planning to send in some of the assigned written work (and/or optional replacement work) to me by this Thursday, May 7th, when our course officially has its last "session," but I do know that I will have to enter a course letter grade for you in the following weeks.

Some of your colleagues in our class have already opted for an arrangement in which I enter a grade of "Incomplete" on May 11th and then, after sufficient quality work has been turned in by a given date (June 1st, for example), I officially change the "Incomplete" to a passing grade of at least B+ (but higher letter grades are still possible).

Others have told me that such an extension (even to July 1st) would not work for them in their current stressful situation and that they would prefer that I give them an actual final passing grade on May 11th (one based on the numerical grade earned at the mid-point in the course on March 12th, plus or minus the quantity and quality of the work done since we all started to shelter in place at home.

I would appreciate your giving your options in this difficult situation some thought and your getting back to me as soon as possible by return email with how you would like for both of us to proceed.

Many thanks – and please be well and stay as healthily productive as you can.

Collegially,

Bob Eidelberg

May 15 / Dear Professor,

I'll be submitting the homework from Saturday today. Is there anything major that I'm missing because I believe I got all the big things. Sorry for not responding so much, I've been having trouble staying motivated during all this chaos.

Maxine

May 18 / From Maxine

I hope you'll accept my two (?) missing assignments with at least partial credit this week. I had to move locations due to family issues so I'm home alone now in Manhattan.

May 23 / Hello, Maxine,

I still have not received from you the two assignments you said were part of the email showing the consent form. I would really like to leave your final grade at A-.

Collegially,

Bob Eidelberg

May 23 / From Maxine

I tried the link again! I don't know why it isn't sending.

May 27 / From Maxine on why she doesn't really want to be reading the required play WAITING FOR GODOT while she's stuck at home during the coronavirus pandemic; it makes her even more stir crazy (though her mother might not mind the assignment),

Although I can see where New York Times theater critic Ben Brantley is coming from when, on March 30, he recommended reading the play "Waiting for Godot" when sheltered in place, I wouldn't necessarily recommend it for readers like me. He agrees that it isn't an escapist work ("but a lot funnier than you may remember") but will make you laugh considering the circumstances. In my opinion, it makes one even more stir crazy for multiple reasons.

First, the repetitive nature of the play is reminiscent of our current coronavirus schedules: we do the same thing every day to the point where we've become sick of the repetition. Wake up, check your phones, look outside, watch TV, make food, happy hour zooms once a week. As a culture that emphasizes the desire to do nothing and be lazy, even we have grown tired of constant television streaming. We don't want something that will make us feel more trapped.

Second, the repetitive dialogue drove me crazy and I truly think this play was meant to be performed and not read. I think I lost a good amount of the significance and humor while trying to read each line and assign it to a person. I think this plot and this dialogue are not something you would read in a time like this, as opposed to when the hustle and bustle is getting to be too much.

However, some people like to brood in their situation and are good with immersing themselves in it. People like my mother might like to feel more stuck or maybe want to relate more to the characters on a deeper level. For those people I say, "Hey, go for it!" It doesn't really affect me what other people read so long as they don't discuss boring topics such as this play in its reading format.

May 27 / Hello, Maxine,

Received at last — and worth the wait! An astute personal response, in particular, to the reading (as opposed to the seeing) of WAITING FOR GODOT. And you've certainly (a carefully chosen word for these times) earned your final course grade of A-.

Stay well!

Collegially,

Bob Eidelberg

May 27 / From Maxine

Thank you very much. I'm disappointed with how the semester ended up but it was a pleasure to take part in your class. It started a lot of interesting philosophical conversations with Ryan over this quarantine, especially the novel "Einstein's Dreams."

Best of luck,

Maxine

Nicole came to the United States in 2003 (I'm not certain from where) and lives in the borough of Queens. Nicole is an upper junior majoring in biology and minoring in psychology; she is not sure of her career goal.

As her email exchanges with me indicate, Nicole had a good deal of trouble adjusting to the demands of distance learning (she apologizes to me for being a "jerk" in a particularly dramatic email), and instead of extending her time any further to finish the course with a grade closer to the "A-" she had earned at the course's on-campus mid-point, Nicole was happy to opt for a final letter grade of "B-." However, I insisted that she accept the "B" she had truly earned for the full 28 sessions.

Portrait of On-Campus Nicole

February 19 / Hey Professor,

Here's my assignment! I forgot to send it yesterday. The email has the date and time it was written (February 18, 4:10 PM), though, since it's a forwarded email. It was done before class started at 5:35 PM, I just didn't get to print it out. I chose the first option, I call the piece "Penelope."

Nicole

Portrait of Distance-Learner Nicole

March 13 / Hello Professor,

Just want to know what work I may be missing and what is due in these coming days now that we won't be attending classes on campus. I'm confused to be honest.

Thanks, I hope you are well.

Nicole

March 13 / Hello Nicole,

You need to now check Blackboard at least twice a week to find any additions or subtractions from the assignments listed in the Calendar of Sessions for Sessions #15 through #20 (plus the due date of March 31 for the work of lit you are reading independently as a member of a group). Following the calendar, everything due gets submitted to the course email on the email itself (not as a pdf) in typing that has been carefully proofread for submission. I hope that clears up any confusion; please know that I will miss hearing your voice in class.

What MAY BE MISSING of yours (I have not yet gone through everyone's submitted written work from Tuesday's class) and which will affect your second-half-of the-course grade is the CW/HW on WAITING FOR LEFTY, the piece of writing inspired by your personal waiting journal entries, the choice of your colleagues' four CW pieces for definite inclusion in our course book SOME DAY, and the additional two (2) submissions I asked for earlier this week on Blackboard about GROWING UP, JACOB AND RACHEL, WAITING FOR LEFTY, etc. So check what you still have at home and send me any and all of those items right away.

Collegially,

Bob Eidelberg

March 18 / From Nicole,

Professor, there's a total of 6 wordy Blackboard announcements. Can you please simplify what is due into a message? I am getting really confused and don't know what I should be doing and your Blackboard announcements just seem to be piling up.

Nicole

March 18 / Hello, Nicole,

I'm sorry that you find all of my six Blackboard announcements so wordy as to be confusing. It would have been helpful to me (to help you) if you had taken the time to be at least a bit specific in your brief email by telling me what you think certain things I wrote meant and asking me whether you were right or at least close to understanding. Since you did not do that, I don't see how my putting all the essential information from the six of them into one message would be of any help to you whatsoever. That "message" would have had to have been quite long to say what was needed to be said and going that route could not have possibly resulted in communication that would have been clearer for you.

So in an attempt to actually be of help to you, let me suggest that you contact by email one of the other students in the class (you were required to have contact information for two of your colleagues by the end of the second week of the course) and ask them to explain the six Blackboard announcements to you since you are the only student in the course to have waited this long to contact me about not understanding pretty much all of what I have been writing to the class since March 11.

I would strongly recommend that you ask the colleague you contact only specific questions for clarification because it would be an imposition to just dump what you seem to imply in your email to me to be total confusion on your part on them and expect them to have the time and patience to interpret everything I have recently sent out to help us all commence distance learning since the last time you were present in class. You should also have in front of you when you call both the handout you received from me at our class's last meeting (which details the Calendar of Sessions for Sessions #15 through #20) and the handout on the independent reading and writing group assignments since most of what I spelled out in my six Blackboard announcements dealt directly with specific changes to be implemented in the content of those two handouts.

All the best in these endeavors.

Collegially,

Bob Eidelberg

March 19 / From Nicole,

So for tonight we have to read ~90 pages of "Waiting for the Barbarians" and submit response prompts that are under #16?

Are we still going to see the Broadway musical "Caroline Or Change"?

Sorry for being a jerk; I'm unhappy and frustrated and I have ADHD and online courses are not suited for me. I am just doing my best right now to not fall behind in this course or drop out.

March 19 / Hello, Nicole,

Thanks for the honest apology and the explanation of why you were being — so surprisingly to me – a jerk.

Hang in there with me and your colleagues as we all work together to manage online distance learning for the remainder of the course. It's new and demanding for all of us.

Also, keep in touch with your contact people and verify with them that you fully understand each Blackboard announcement and assignment every Wednesday and Friday. There's no shame in that — and be a colleague in return. Your understanding of what to write about under Session #16 is essentially correct, so get to it because it's due tonight (if you are a bit late this time, I won't hold it against you, but that is only a one-time concession).

Officially, our trip to see CAROLINE, OR CHANGE is off because all Broadway theaters are now closed to at least the middle of April, and group sales is planning on soon refunding me the full $1,100 cost of the tickets. However, if the Broadway theaters open again before our course ends, I will do my best to get free tickets for a performance we can all go to together.

Collegially,

Bob Eidelberg

March 25 / Hey Professor,

Thank you for the extension; it's greatly appreciated. I saw your last Blackboard post and want to explain my personal situation to you.

I have ADHD and it's hard to deal with; concentrating and getting things done is not easy for me. On top of all this, I'm POOR. My family immigrated to this country, we are POOR. I live in a 2-bedroom with 4 other family members. I share a room with my cousin. In this tiny space, it's hard to get anything done. Plus my family is Hispanic and LOUD. Before all of this, I was at Baruch library until 12 am at least 4 days a week to get my work done. I need you to please be patient with me.

I'm attaching a picture of the makeshift desk I just came up with next to the stove in our kitchen and think it will help. I want you to know that I am trying my best, but it's hard.

April 9 / Hello, groupmates for the novel THE AGE OF INNOCENCE,

Are any of you in the process of finishing up on your essay about THE AGE OF INNOCENCE?

All of the five other groups have fairly fully reported in and their work has been reproduced by me for Chapter 15 of our course's book SOME DAY.

Weird — but I don't have a word in that chapter on the Edith Wharton novel, which is not only a literary shame but an inexplicable class anomaly!

So, would ALL OF YOU get back to me one way or the other on the answer to the question of whether any of you is finishing up an essay?

Collegially,

Bob Eidelberg

April 9 / Hey Professor,

I'm almost there.

Nicole

April 13 / Hey Professor,

My family members are sick now and I'm not in a good place at the moment. It's been very difficult to get anything done. I was wondering if I'd be able to ask for a final grade of Incomplete. I'm doing all the work, just not at the pace that everyone is. If that's not doable, would you recommend dropping the class?

Nicole

April 13 / Hello, Nicole,

Sorry to hear about your "not being in a good place right now" (understandable!) and your family's health problems.

Since you say that you are doing all the work but not at the pace of most of your colleagues (and I have no reason not to accept that), why don't we both see where you are at the beginning of May? I could give you on May 1 an unofficial letter grade by email based on everything you had completed by then (regardless of when each piece was turned in), and if that letter grade worked for you, then you could authorize me to enter it.

Otherwise, we would then go for the "Incomplete," and that could be changed to a letter grade by me at the end of August, let's say.

What do you think of these several options? (And this is important: it's a "no" advice from me to your dropping the course — you were running a B+/A- at the mid-point of the course; so that would be, shall we both say, a "jerk" thing for you to do at this late point in time.)

Collegially,

Bob Eidelberg

April 14 / Professor,

Thank you for being so kind and accommodating, professor. I spoke to my therapist today and things feel a little better. This message is definitely cherry on top. I'm gonna get to reading now. Thank you. Please remain in good health.

Nicole

May 3 / Hello, Colleagues Who Have Been Privately Bcc'd This Personal Email,

Please give the email below your close attention. Thank you.

Collegially,

Bob Eidelberg

Begin forwarded message:

Hello,

It's been a while since I have heard from you either by a response to an email of mine, a Blackboard request, or a significant number of homework assignments turned in (even late), and I am concerned about your physical and mental health and your anxiety status during these worrisome times.

Also, I don't know whether you are doing any of the currently required reading in our "Literature of Waiting" course and are planning to send in some of the assigned written work (and/or optional replacement work) to me by this Thursday, May 7th, when our course officially has its last "session," but I do know that I will have to enter a course letter grade for you in the following weeks.

Some of your colleagues in our class have already opted for an arrangement in which I enter a grade of "Incomplete" on May 11th and then, after sufficient quality work has been turned in by a given date (June

1st, for example), I officially change the "Incomplete" to a passing grade of at least B+ (but higher letter grades are still possible).

Others have told me that such an extension (even to July 1st) would not work for them in their current stressful situation and that they would prefer that I give them an actual final passing grade on May 11th (one based on the numerical grade earned at the mid-point in the course on March 12th, plus or minus the quantity and quality of the work done since we all started to shelter in place at home.

I would appreciate your giving your options in this difficult situation some thought and your getting back to me as soon as possible by return email with how you would like for both of us to proceed.

Many thanks – and please be well and stay as healthily productive as you can.

Collegially,

Bob Eidelberg

May 7 / Hi,

Sorry, professor. I've been working daily at a testing site to pay rent. I think I can get things done by mid-June?

Nicole

Friday, May 8 ("The Literature of Waiting" course had its last "session" on May 7 / Hello, Nicole,

Truly sorry to hear that your life is still so stressed. As you are no doubt aware, several of your colleagues in the class are working and living under similar or worse pandemic constraints. As far as how you and I proceed from here, the options you have need to be in line with the arrangements I have made in the past two weeks with those other students in our class.

So, since you had an A- at the mid-point of the term but have turned in no work since then, if I get your piece on THE AGE OF INNOCENCE by the middle of next week, you can get a B- for the course. However, if you want to work for a mark of B, or B+ or even as high as the A- you were running on March 10, then you need to submit on an ongoing basis missing and/ or replacement quality work over the next several weeks, but with the last piece of work you submit in my hands by June 1.

Please let me know within the next day or two at the most how you want to proceed.

Collegially,

Bob Eidelberg

Monday, May 11 / From Nicole

I'll submit my "Age of Innocence" work by Wednesday. I think this is the best option for me. Thank you and so sorry to disappoint. This semester was a nightmare.

Nicole

Monday, May 11 / Hello, Nicole,

Okay, Nicole, and if your piece on THE AGE OF INNOCENCE is really good and in my hands by this Wednesday afternoon at the latest, I might be able to justify a B instead of a B- for the course grade.

Also, you must send me right away the signed consent form for our course book SOME DAY, or everything will still be up in the air.

I hope the next several weeks work out well for you at work and at home. Take care.

Collegially,

Bob Eidelberg

Thursday, May 14 / Hello Professor,

Can I please hand in the essay on Friday the 15ᵗʰ? Unfortunately I overestimated my abilities when I emailed you and didn't think about how Wednesday was only two days away and how behind and out of practice I am with my writing. I've read the novels but am in need of today to fully construct my ideas and figure out how to get them on paper.

I've written and backspaced so much writing, it's killing me. I feel like my writing is too subjective.

I find myself second-guessing the following:

Is it okay if I use words like "I" in my essay?

Is it okay if one of the reasons I wish to include Edith Wharton's "The Age of Innocence" is the fact that the author is a woman and seems to give more life to Ellen than the other two male writers do with any of their female characters? Ellen is just so much more three-dimensional. She's imperfect, but likable. In contrast, the women in Ha Jin and Coetzee's worlds often felt like burdens, nags, weak. But then Archer kind of does this with May, so I contradict myself.

Is it okay if one of the reasons I want to include "The Age of Innocence" rather than "Waiting for the Barbarians" is simply that it was more enticing/a better read for me?

Is it okay if one of the reasons I want to include "The Age of Innocence" is its NY setting? And how I think it's a good novel to read alongside Ha Jin's "Waiting" because of the romance aspect?

I still wish to applaud "Waiting for the Barbarians" in my essay for effectively illustrating paranoia and dread, a feeling that many of us have learned very well while we wait for this pandemic to be over, if it ever will be over. Still, I want to make it clear I want it to be replaced. Is it appropriate to mention the pandemic in my essay or the effect it had on my reading of these novels?

I also feel like a reason I wish to exclude "Waiting for the Barbarians" from the course is because of the weird massaging this much older man is performing on a blind young girl who he speaks of as if she was a child.

And I grew further disturbed by his descriptions of her emptiness, but still, he does this every day? I just grew really annoyed at the main character and came to dislike him because of how he treated the girl, doing with her what he wants. The back and forth?

But still, I feel like one of the reasons I wish for "The Age of Innocence" to replace "Waiting for the Barbarians" is because I didn't like the latter very much, but is this too dismissive?

In addition, I think it'd be helpful to hear about what you wonder as you read the above? What questions am I not answering? What details/thoughts would you like me to expand? What would you like to see more of?

Thank you for extending the B offer, by the way. I wish I had been able to carry that out, but honestly I am grateful for a B-.

Sorry for such a ridiculous email; I don't often find myself stuck like this.

Nicole

May 14 / Hello, Nicole,

I just now finished reading this email of yours — it is not at all ridiculous (actually, it's highly reflective) and if your essay (yes to "I," since It's a personal essay, not a formal persuasive one) includes all of the areas you want my thoughts about, it is going to be superb and I can't wait to read it (don't worry about how long it might turn out to be); in fact, I can wait; since I am getting back to you so late and I don't want to further stress you out, send the essay to me on Sunday afternoon the 17th of May rather than this Friday the 15th, okay?

Collegially,

Bob Eidelberg

May 17 / From Nicole,

I sent you my essay with drive and then remembered you can only accept pdf format. I just got home from work, here is the pdf. I will be checking out this consent form you're talking about.

May 17 / From Nicole,

Thank you for being really nice, professor. Your willingness to work with me truly makes me want to be better and I just feel very blessed. Thank you. I hope you enjoy your time off and continue to remain in good health.

Also, now that our course is over; if you or anyone you know needs antibody testing done, I work at a free antibody testing site in Sunset Park.

Jason, who lives in the borough of Queens and commutes to Hunter by subway, is an upper sophomore majoring in economics and minoring in computer science, with plans to become an "analyst."

In our on-campus sessions, Jason was a highly engaged and insightful participant and, in fact, was the first student to volunteer to be called on, Day 1, establishing his pattern of commentary both thoughtful and thought-provoking. A major contributor of creative writing in the forms of mini-plays and poems, Jason earned a final letter grade of "A+" in our course on "The Literature of Waiting."

Portrait of On-Campus Jason

February 6 / Hey Professor,

I writing this email to send to you my letter with the song that relates to waiting. I noticed on the syllabus that this email address is not to send any late assignments and I totally understand that. I am sending you my assignment selfishly as it would eat me up inside if I didn't even try. There might be a parallel here to our class discussion about the "The Trial" here somewhere. I understand if you don't look over it, it was my fault for not bringing it in printed. Anyways, thank you for your time, and sorry for the wait.

February 8 / Hello, Jason,

You had me at "it would eat me up inside if I didn't even try." And you clinched it with the definite (not just "might be") parallel to our class discussion on THE TRIAL.

Can't wait to more than "look it over." See you Tuesday.

Collegially,

Bob Eidelberg

P.S. How come so quiet in class after such a fine start on Day 1?

February 8 / Hey again, Professor,

Thank you again for your time, I truly do appreciate it. I was really hoping not to be asked the question you asked in your postscript, but the least I can do is give you an honest answer, as embarrassing as it is.

The reason for my silence on Tuesday was due to me being childishly upset that my poem didn't get chosen as one of the seven. You also left two sets of question marks on my poem. The first set was where I wrote "for see"; the reason I wrote that was since the words we were allowed to use were limited I decided to substitute the word "forsee" for "for see." The second set was when on the last stanza, as well as you correcting my use of the word "to" to "too." I used "to" because I believe "too" doesn't appear in the story, therefore, not a usable word. To briefly explain my last stanza, it's about how when you're waiting for a change for the better to occur in life but you take no action other than waiting, nothing better will happen. It depicts a bad situation getting worse ("it is now getting darker and darker") due to inaction and how you will only feel sorry for waiting because it will be so dark that you will no longer even be able to see. During class I wanted to ask you what the criteria were for how you chose the seven poems; however, I immediately realized that would be incredibly insensitive to the seven that were chosen. It also made me wonder about how the others who also worked hard felt that their work wasn't good enough to get chosen. If they felt as frustrated as me. This ultimately ended up with me saying nothing at all, and for the entirety of class it weighed on my mind. I decided that I would bring it up after class or in an email, but as soon as class was dismissed, it seemed so insignificant. I believed that I wrote a good poem and was proud of my work and that's all that mattered. If only I came to that breakthrough at the start of class, and not after. Also, it should have been obvious to me that, of course, you wouldn't see my poem as clearly as I did, especially considering I had to explain some aspects here. Moving forward, I will try not to be so grammatically abstract, or at the very least I will add some explanation.

As for Thursday, my silence was simply a result of feeling ashamed that I didn't turn in my assignment. As well as thinking of what I would be able to do to atone for it. In my mind, I was face to face with my own gatekeeper. If I should accept that what's done is done and to forever wait outside, wondering what could've been if I tried something different, or to just force my way past him. My gatekeeper being my own conscious and ideals and knowing that by sending you my assignment that I am not only breaking your written rules on the syllabus but as well selfishly giving my assignment in with an unfair two-hour extension. However, I decided to send you my assignment as a way of settling my own thoughts and to silence any thoughts that would have started with "what if," I would've had later on. That class discussion on Thursday truly did feel like the universe was mocking me; however, it did help me gain the courage to go beyond my gatekeeper, and do something I would've had never thought about doing in any other situation.

Once again, I cannot thank you enough for your time.

Sincerely,

Jason

February 24 / Hey Professor,

I know "The Dumb Waiter" is over and done with in class but I've thought of something that I'd like to share with you. In the play, Gus says that he got the saying "Light the gas" from his mother and sticks to this despite how increasingly aggressive Ben gets. From the comedic communication assignment from the previous class, I spoke to Ryan of our class and he noted the part where there is a callback to this figure of speech gag at the end of the play when Ben is speaking into the serving hatch's voice tube. In the callback it goes:

Ben (Excitedly): Did you hear that?

Gus: What?

Ben: You know what he said? Light the kettle! Not put on the kettle! Not light the gas! But light the kettle!

The person speaking to Ben, most likely a higher up in the organization, can be seen as an authority figure to both Ben and Gus. Ben finds so much joy in being able to be proven correct by this authority figure and as such uses the same figure of speech. What this shows is that Gus holds his mother's figure of speech in higher regard to the figure of speech used by not only his senior partner but the authority figure that governs both his senior partner and himself. Perhaps this could be a reason as to why Gus felt so distraught over the job with the previous girl. Gus's affinity for women would be a result of his mother who he views as an absolute authority, which is shown through this gag.

Thank you for reading.

Jason

Portrait of Distance-Learner Jason

March 14 / Hey Professor,

I hope all is well during these trying times. I apologize for my absence on Tuesday as I was feeling sick and didn't want to chance anything by coming in. Here are some of the assignments I owe you, I hope you get around to reading them, in particular my assignment based on "Waiting for Lefty." Please be safe and I'm looking forward to seeing how we continue with our class.

March 19 / Hey Professor,

I hope you are doing well. Attached is my assignment. Please take care.

March 22 / Hey Professor,

Got your e-mail, attached is the found poem. Take care.

March 22 / Hey Professor,

Attached is my coda for "The Dumb Waiter." Take care.

March 26 / Hey Professor,

Attached is the assignment due for Session 17. Take care.

March 31 / Hey Professor,

Attached is my assignment for Session 18 as well as my poem. I felt like I really nailed the last stanza for my poem and I hope you think so as well. Hope all is well, do take care.

April 2 / Hello, Jason,

What a clever, well-written, economically factual and wise piece of writing (with allusions to THE DUMB WAITER as well as riffing off of WAITING FOR LEFTY).

It is nothing to sneeze at (!), and I can't wait to use your "waiting game" dramatic scene "Gesundheit" in our course's book SOME DAY. But I need to get it from you on a clickable pdf icon. Possible?

Collegially,

Bob Eidelberg

April 3 / Hey Professor,

Attached is my essay on "Rosencrantz and Guildenstern Are Dead." Take care.

April 7 / Hey Professor,

Attached is my assignment for Session 20. Hope all is well.

April 9 / Hey Professor,

Attached is the script for my marriage therapy session. Take care.

April 22 / Hey Professor,

Please pardon the egregiously late assignments. I have got to admit I'm not exactly handling the whole quarantining situation mentally as well as I had expected. My other classes also just so happen to be bombarding me with exams, which honestly feels like some sort of collusion against me right about now. However, I understand this doesn't excuse my lateness, and I'm terribly sorry for the inconvenience. I hope all is well on your end!

P.S. I'm looking forward to giving options 3 and 4 of the last session my best shot!

April 23 / Hey guys in my group,

Attached is my assignment for Session 24 featuring "Stressed Out" by Twenty One Pilots. Hope everyone's doing alright.

April 28 / Hey Professor,

Attached is my assignment for Session 25. I hope all is well.

May 2 / Hey Professor,

I hope all is well. Attached is my assignment for Session 26. "Waiting for Godot" really is some serious business.

May 3 / Hey Professor,

Attached is my consent form for our course book; if there are any issues please let me know.

The address I will leave below should match the one you already have; if I end up typing something different below than what you already have, please go with the address you already have on file and had used to mail me the class schedule two months ago.

May 3 / Hey Professor,

I was just curious as to what my grade is for the course as well as if I happen to be missing any assignments. Please let me know and I will do my best to address it. Thank you for your time. Stay well.

May 4 / Hey Professor,

It turns out that I completely missed the CW piece that was supposed to be based on the 10 Waiting Journal entries due a while ago. So to answer your question, I have 10 Waiting Journals, and attached to this email will be my CW piece. Sorry about that. Also, I believe I sent my "Waiting For Godot" assignment with the subject line "Session 26 Assignment" on May 2nd. However, I will attach it to this email regardless. Thank you for your time and sorry about the wait.

May 5 / Hey Professor,

Attached is my assignment for Session 27. Stay well.

May 6 / Hey Professor,

I received your email earlier today and just wanted to make sure if everything was clear on my consent form. Also as for the returning of the Coursepack, I plan on returning it when the fall semester starts. If you need anything else, such as assignments, from me please let me know. Stay well.

May 7 / Hey Professor,

Attached is my assignment for Session 28. Take care.

Gabriella is an upper sophomore majoring in history and planning on becoming a teacher. She lives in the borough of Manhattan and commutes to Hunter College by subway. Health issues caused Gabriella to be absent from four out of our class's first thirteen sessions, but Gabriella always immediately made up the work she had missed, and was running an A- grade at the mid-point of the course on March 10 when distance learning commenced.

Being sheltered at home and learning remotely did not go well for Gabriella; she fell badly behind in her reading and writing during the rest of March and well into April, but then Gabriella, as the narrative arc of her emails indicates, began making up assignment after assignment (as well as doing five extra credit projects) so that by our last remote session on May 7, Gabriella had fully earned the "A" she received from me in the course.

Portrait of On-Campus and Distance-Learner Gabriella

March 30 / Hello, Gabriella,

Are you doing okay? I'm concerned because I have not heard back from you in response to the three or four emails I have sent – from both our course email and my personal email – over the past week and a half, and I remember that you were feeling under the weather in the last week or so of our on-campus classes.

Please let me know that you have received this email and that all (or most of life) is well.

Collegially,

Bob Eidelberg

In response to the early impact of the coronavirus pandemic on our now completely off-campus student body, certain members of the administration of Hunter College emailed a communication to their faculty with the advisement that they notify students of Hunter's online counseling services and encourage those we thought might be in need. I immediately forwarded that email to about a third of my class.

April 3 / Hello, Colleagues,

Don't be hesitant to contact them if you are in need (see "Counseling for Students" email below).

Collegially,

Bob Eidelberg

Begin forwarded message:

Subject: Counseling for students
Date: April 3, 2020 at 8:44:27 AM EDT

As the pandemic continues, more people are experiencing the loss of loved ones. Some of these people are our students — some of you may already have heard from students whose relatives have died. It goes without saying that we should all treat them with sensitivity, flexibility, and consideration.

There is counseling available to students who want it. Counseling and Wellness Services is operating remotely at this time. Please encourage students to call their main number at 212.772.4931 to set up an appointment when they are ready. They are checking voicemail remotely and are responding to students within the business day. Students should also feel free to email them at personalcounseling@hunter.cuny.edu. The first step in their process is to schedule a phone meeting, which is typically scheduled within a day of a student's first outreach to them.

April 11 / Dear Professor Eidelberg,

I hope that you are doing well. I have fallen very far behind in class, because of some personal and mental health issues that have made it very difficult for me to keep up with school work. I know it would have been better if I reached out sooner, however part of what I have been struggling with is getting motivated to do things that are important to me. This class is truly important to me and I want to know the best way to make up the work. I would really appreciate some guidance on how best to make up past work. Thank you so much for your understanding.

Best,

Gabriella

April 21 / Dear Professor Eidelberg,

I hope this email finds you well and that you are staying healthy during the coronavirus. I emailed you last week about my absence, but it appears that I was not diligent enough and sent it to the wrong email. This email is forwarded from my previous email. Succinctly, I have had a very hard time adjusting to at-home learning and had a very bad episode for my mental health. I am now trying to get myself back on track. Attached I have many of the assignments that I missed and I will make sure to send you the rest of my assignments.

Thank you so much for your understanding.

Best,

Gabriella

April 21 / Hello, Gabriella,

Welcome back! I am so glad to hear from you and so sorry that you have been having a bad time of it. I suspected as much and even personally emailed you a few times, but I don't know whether you got any of those emails as I was always told that I had the wrong (undeliverable) email address (it was the same email address as the one you just emailed me from, so I don't know what's going on!).

In any case, I am encouraged by what you say about trying to get yourself back on track and by the high quality of the assignments you have attached, it looks as if you are succeeding. Don't overdue it, please, as you go forward with the assignments for the rest of the course. It's more than okay to be a bit late.

By the way, did you receive the optional "make-up" assignment pages for our last session on May 7th? Let me know, and if you didn't, I will resend those pages to you.

Stay well, be calm, be kind, stay sane!

Collegially,

Bob Eidelberg

April 23 / From Gabriella to her groupmates on the novel GREAT EXPECTATIONS,

I was so excited to have the chance to read a classic like GREAT EXPECTATIONS because I had never read it or any other Dickens in school. GREAT EXPECTATTIONS was beautifully written, and the scenes were evocative. I felt myself in the room with Miss Havisham ... and I sneezed from all the dust that accumulated on her belongings.

April 23 / From Gabriella to her poetry groupmates (and to Professor Eidelberg) on her choice of a "waiting" poem,

Good morning. Here is my poem. I hope everyone is staying safe.

April 23 / Dear Professor,

Here is my "waiting" song. I wrote it with a tune in my head, so I hope it translates.

Best,

Gabriella

May 6 / Dear Professor Eidelberg,

Here are some of the homework and extra credit pieces. I will be sending more soon.

I hope you are staying healthy!

Best,

Gabriella

May 7 / Dear Professor,

I hope you have a good night. Here are two more extra credit assignments. I think I have caught up, but I was wondering if you could tell me if I am missing anything? Thank you so much.

Best,

Gabriella

May 11 / From Mr. Eidelberg,

Thank you so much, Gabriella, for these pieces – they were all insightful, imaginative, and well-written – and several of your extra credit pieces will be published in our course's book SOME DAY. However, in order for you to be credited by name, you need to send me your signed consent form right away.

Many thanks. Stay well.

May 13 / Hi Professor,

I'm sorry that everything has taken longer than planned. Here is the consent form. Hope you have a great summer!

Thank you for an amazing and interesting semester.

Best,

Gabriella

May 14 / Hello, Gabriella,

I may have already responded to this email since I know I received these two further extra credit assignments and gave you high marks for them. I looks like you've more than earned your "A" in the course.

Be well.

Collegially,

Bob Eidelberg

May 18 / Dear Professor Eidelberg,

Thank you so much! It was a joy learning in your class. I hope you have a great and healthy summer.

Best,

Gabriella

Wardah wanted to be known as and called on in class as "Malik," her last name. Malik lives on Long Island, in Westbury, New York, and is a lower junior majoring in psychology who doesn't know yet what profession she would like to go into. Shy about and unaccustomed to participating in class during the first half of the course, Malik rose to the challenge of insightful and creative writing once the course, at its mid-point, went into distance learning. Malik earned an on-time final letter grade of "A."

Portrait of On-Campus Wardah

January 29 / From Malik,

Hi my name is Malik, which is my last, not my first, name, but I prefer to be called it. I'm in your English 25146 class, I'm sorry I couldn't make it yesterday, I've been sick for a few days and I wasn't sure what email address I can tell you that on but I will be there tomorrow!

February 12 / Hi Professor,

I need a copy of the play THE DUMB WAITER, I forgot mine at the train station! Thank you.

February 13 / Hi Professor,

I wanted to say this in class but we changed topics and I had this all written out but I had to wait (ha!) for the train to have service again. But another way Ben in THE DUMB WAITER has a sense of order in his life is self-control, he knows he can't control his environment or what happens but as long as he has his tea and does his ritual his own self of mind will be okay, does that make sense?

February 13 / Hello, Malik,

It makes quite a lot of sense – and one of us should bring this point up in class at our next session, okay?

Collegially,

Bob Eidelberg

February 13 / Hello, Malik,

I put a mimeographed copy of the Harold Pinter play in the regular mail to you tonight so you should have it at your home address by no later than Tuesday's mail.

Collegially,

Bob Eidelberg

Portrait of Distance-Learner Wardah

March 26 / Hi Professor,

I don't have a printer to print out the consent form for my work to be published in our course's book SOME DAY, so I can't sign it and don't know how I can mail it to you! So is there any other way to do it?

March 26 / Hello, Malik

I didn't know that and, quite frankly, hadn't thought of it as a possibility, but there is another more traditional way how to do this: you can copy the consent form out by hand — word for word — on a piece of lined paper, which you would then sign and date and mail back to me at my home address (it's on the form) through the regular mail.

Sounds good?

Collegially,

Bob Eidelberg

April 6 / To my fellow group members reading the Daniel Defoe novel
ROBINSON CRUSOE,

I agree with you that people wait to interact with others and everyone needs human interaction. Sometimes lack of hope and desperation is what drives people to break out of their situation, and I think ROBINSON CRUSOE portrays that anything is possible. I think this book also shows how to survive during a traumatizing time and that some things that we want we don't need. A spiritual awakening is a type of waiting, he had to look inward.

April 6 / Hello, Malik,

Whose piece on ROBINSON CRUSOE are you responding to? Can you forward it to me since I don't seem to have it?

Collegially,

Bob Eidelberg

April 7 / Hi Professor,

I was responding to Gamal's, and will send it to you.

April 22 / From Malik,

I'm so sorry, professor, that I haven't been able to hand in my homework, it's been a stressful week for me but is it okay if I send in yesterday's homework by Friday, or will I get points off or anything?

Thank you!

April 22 / Hello, Malik,

Not a problem, Malik; late homeworks are our new normal.

Collegially,

Bob Eidelberg

Carolyn is an upper sophomore who lives in the borough of Queens and commutes by subway to Hunter College in upper Manhattan. Carolyn is majoring in human biology and hopes to become a doctor.

Before she lost her job when all of New York City's restaurants got officially closed down because of the coronavirus pandemic, Carolyn worked as a waitress. Having registered late for our course in "The Literature of Waiting," Carolyn missed the first two sessions of the class and part of the third but was not absent again until every one of us got ourselves absented from the Hunter campus after Session #13 on March 10. Carolyn excelled during distance learning and earned a final course letter grade of "A+."

Portrait of On-Campus Carolyn

February 5 / From Carolyn,

Hello, what are the requirements for the song letter?

Portrait of Distance-Learner Carolyn

March 11 / From Carolyn,

Hello Professor, not sure if you received my other email because it's been loading for some time but I was wondering if we will be emailing the assignment or what's going to happen because online they were discussing a recess from class coming up.

March 17 / From Carolyn,

Session 15 work attached. I have also emailed you from a different email with Thursday's work and saying that I have no one's contact information, but haven't gotten a response from you. So, not sure if you've received my work.

March 24 / Hello, Selected Colleagues,

For the chapter in our course book SOME DAY on the CW/HW you did in connection with the short story "A Telephone Call," please send me (but only on a pdf attachment to an email, please) your first-rate creative piece in connection with Dorothy Parker's story.

Collegially,

Bob Eidelberg

March 24 / From Carolyn,

Which exactly is the hw you're asking for from that piece?

March 24 / Hello, Carolyn,

It was the creative writing in which you either extended Dorothy Parker's short story, or wrote it from the young man's point of view instead of from the young woman's, or wrote it about something connecting people other than realistic or romantic love. If you can't locate it, that's okay.

Collegially,

Bob Eidelberg

March 24 / From Carolyn,

Thank you, I handed mine to you after class the week before our last meeting on campus. It's an extension with five sentences, just an extension from her point of view, do you maybe have that?

March 25 / From Mr. Eidelberg,

Thanks, Carolyn. I found it, and it's quite good.

April 11 / From Carolyn,

Hello. "Wizard of Oz" work. Hope all is good.

April 12 From Mr. Eidelberg,

Hello, Carolyn. I'm very much intrigued by the idea you had for a fourth character to join Dorothy on the journey that takes them all to see the wizard. Why don't you give it a try in a creative piece of writing that lets us readers know who or what that character is and what idea or quality your created character is meant to represent in the story.

April 13 / From Carolyn,

Thanks, I did give it a try.

April 13 / Hello, Carolyn,

And you succeeded! It's definitely a candidate for inclusion in our course's book SOME DAY.

Collegially,

Bob Eidelberg

April 14 / From Carolyn,

Thank you so much!

May 5 / From Carolyn,

Hello, attached is the work due tomorrow. Also I just noticed the announcement for the journals – are we supposed to just have ten or send you ten?

May 5 / From Mr. Eidelberg,

You're fine on keeping for yourself all of the personal waiting journal entries you wrote, but you do need to send me very soon your signed (and home-addressed) consent form for our course's book SOME DAY.

Collegially,

Bob Eidelberg

May 5 / From Carolyn,

Okay, thank you!

Chyna is an upper sophomore who has not yet chosen a major; she was an extremely quiet student both in class and during distance learning. Although Chyna has three email addresses, it was never quite clear to me (or, I discovered, to her!) which of the three was working properly at any given time. Consequently, although Chyna apparently missed a good many of my personally directed emails, she did manage to complete "The Literature of Waiting" course on time with a final letter grade of "A" by faithfully following my online Blackboard announcements and by doing several extra credit projects.

Portrait of On-Campus and Distance-Learner Chyna

March 22 / Hello, Chyna,

I am sending this email as a direct reply ON your email sent by phone. For some reason, apparently none (or, at best, only a couple) of my emails are getting through to you and I always use the email I see on the emails you send me. If you get this email, can you write me back from another email address that you have? Or can you suggest what the problem might be? And is anyone else having the same problem (that you have been made aware of)?

Collegially,

Bob Eidelberg

March 22 / Good Evening,

I definitely received your email and this is definitely the better option to receive any messages. I have not been sending homework or additional assignments due to the emails and notifications being sent out about Hunter's classes not starting until March 19th. All of my other classes began on that date which is why I assumed our class would do the same. I believed the time was for professors to change their syllabus or extend midterms. My apologies but I had not checked our Blackboard announcements because I believed there was no reason to. Now that I have read all the emails and prompts I understand your waiting to receive my assignments. I haven't missed any assignments before this and hopefully can send in missing work due to the confusion.

April 3 / Good Evening,

*Due to a close passing in my family and someone in my house being sick it took longer for me to send everything (and me being the only child) and I apologize for that. If **anything** is missing or done wrongly please let me know. Apologies for the inconvenience to you but I am adjusting taking care of someone and making time for your assignments, that still remains important to me.*

May 6 / Good Evening Professor,

It has been a little difficult sending the assignments on time due to my time being taken up by caring for my father; however I definitely will proceed to send the work in full and I will be sending Session 27 shortly.

Paige is an upper freshman who lives in the Bronx and commutes to Hunter by subway. She is majoring in social psychology. Paige was a relatively quiet student during our on-campus class discussions (perhaps because of her age and freshman status); however, she was a diligent reader, perceptive academic writer, and imaginative contributor to our course's book SOME DAY.

On the next to the last day of our distance learning class, Paige wondered in an email to me whether she should take an Incomplete and use the time to do extra credit creative writing on the course's theme. I informed her that she had already earned an "A" in the course.

Portrait of On-Campus and Distance-Learner Paige

March 21 / Hello, Selected Colleagues,

I hope you and your loved ones are doing well; I have a favor to ask of you in these chaotic times. I would like to include in our course's book SOME DAY the first-rate work you did (a 95 or higher mark) on the several creative writing pieces you wrote earlier in the semester and up to the end of our on-campus class.

So, if you can, please send me within the next few days a pdf of any of those pieces that you would like to be considered for publication, such as the Kate Croy found poem, the letter to a friend inspired by a song, the coda to THE DUMB WAITER, the changes you made in the vignettes to WAITING FOR LEFTY, the creative writing you did in connection with WAITING, and especially, your "How to Be a Waiter" piece.

Many thanks. Stay well and calm, sane and productive, caring and kind to others.

Collegially,

Bob Eidelberg

March 24 / Hello, Paige,

Please put this on a pdf attachment to an email; I am not electronically able to access any of your first-rate CW/HW that I'll be requesting when it is an integral part of the email you send.

Many thanks.

Collegially,

Bob Eidelberg

March 24 / From Paige,

I don't understand. How do I do that?

March 24 / Hello, Paige,

Oh! I don't think I can properly teach you how to do this. Could you reach out by phone to one of your group colleagues who is more computer savvy than either you or I and ask them for help with this?

Collegially,

Bob Eidelberg

March 24 / From Paige,

Alrighty I will. Thank you!

March 25 / From Paige,

I hope this is the correct method.

March 25 / Thanks, but sorry, Paige,

This separation alone does not constitute a pdf attachment to an email. Let me send you — in a few minutes – an email that I've received from another student where you can access the pdf attachment icon at the bottom of the email. When you click on the icon, voila! — the attachment is now printed out in the form I need for getting your CW/HW pieces into our course's book.

Collegially,

Bob Eidelberg

April 5 / From Carolyn to Paige and the other HHH groupmates (and to Professor Eidelberg),

I enjoyed Paige's essay on the novel by Shirley Jackson – "The Haunting of Hill House." I feel she expressed her ideas in a good style, and it was well-written. She also brought up a lot of points that I recognized but hadn't really noticed as ways they specifically waited throughout the day by eating and playing board games, so I liked that she pointed that out. I also agreed on what was said on the Coetzee piece because I also did not enjoy it and found it hard to follow/understand the narrator overall. I also like that she fit in how we can take the book further by taking those extra steps with creative writing to make an extended ending, which the book leaves various opportunities for because it ends kind of in a cliff hanger and leaves you wondering how the other characters continued their life and dealt with Eleanor's death and what happens with the house itself. Paige was able to really point out how the characters waited and how therefore the author left us the audience also waiting for night to fall and paranormal activity to occur, which was interesting and created suspense. Overall, I agree with everything mentioned in Paige's essay and how she got her point across and how this was an easier reading to follow and keep up with, and so I would definitely want to get rid of "Waiting for the Barbarians" and replace it with this novel instead.

April 14 / Perceptive responses, Paige,

To all four questions you dealt with, but I am particularly impressed by your musings on why author L. Frank Baum in THE WIZARD OF OZ chose the traits that he did for the three characters that wind up joining Dorothy on her way to see the Wizard. I hope you go for the option of creating a fourth character in a CW/HW, particularly because your excellent musings were instigated by that extra credit assignment.

Collegially,

Bob Eidelberg

May 6 / Good Afternoon Mr. Eidelberg,

I am considering taking an incomplete grade for this course. However, is it possible for you to tell me my current standing in the course?

Sincerely,

Paige

Note from the instructor:

Although one of the shyer students in the class during our thirteen on-campus sessions, Paige decided to take the "complete" letter grade of an "A" after I informed her by email that she had earned that grade from the high quality of her written work all semester, including three replacement pieces for missing assignments and several extra credit projects.

Hester is living in Manhattan while attending Hunter College as a visiting student from Arizona State University; she is an upper junior majoring in English. Hester's active and perceptive participation in class discussions during the first thirteen sessions of our course on "The Literature of Waiting" and her generally solid written homework earned her an A- at the mid-point in the course.

Although Hester seemed initially thrown by the ways and means of distance learning, she rallied well in the last weeks of the semester with top grades on her analytical pieces of the literature under study and with several extra credit creative writing projects to maintain her A- as her final course grade.

Our email correspondence during a period in distance learning when Hester was not submitting work to me was, however, technically something out of the theater of the absurd (which the class was actually studying via Beckett and Pinter).

Portrait of On-Campus Hester

February 12 / Hello Professor,

As I will not be in class tomorrow, I have sent you my homework in advance.

Thank you!

Hester

February 17 / Hello Mr. Eidelberg,

Not only is Homer's Penelope clever and cunning, biding her time and fending off countless suitors as she awaits her husband Odysseus's return, there is an assertion (primarily by feminist critics) that she is, in fact, furious. Her calculating nature demonstrates her intelligence and patience. I've attached for you and for possible sharing with my colleagues in the class Dorothy Parker's 1982 poem "Penelope."

Hester

180

February 18 / Hello, Hester,

Thanks for the info on the Dorothy Parker piece.

March 4 / Hi Professor,

After double checking my schedule, I realized that March 22 as one of the possible dates for our class trip to see the Broadway musical CAROLINE, OR CHANGE is a date that works for me. Thought I'd let you know as to not further influence any decision-making on your part.

Thank you!

Hester

Portrait of Distance-Learner Hester

March 19 / Dear Professor,

Unfortunately, I lost the handout with all our next several sessions' prompt questions. If you are able to send me them, I will complete them and email them to you by tomorrow. (If not, I understand!)

Hester

March 22 / From Hester,

I sent this email Thursday. I just wanted to double-check after reading your Blackboard announcement that I was emailing the right person.

March 24 / Hello, Hester,

Have you checked both your recent spam and suspect emails? I've emailed you the calendar of our remote sessions twice now (actually from my personal email instead of our course email, as I cannot seem to mail it successfully to you at any of your three (3!) email addresses using our course email). I'll send it out once more, but if you somehow don't get it, try calling a colleague in the class to read the relevant parts over the phone to you or to send it all from their phone. How does that sound?

Collegially,

Bob Eidelberg

March 24 / From Hester

Hi, just checking back in as I still do not have access to the calendar of sessions.

Would you mind emailing me them? They are not in the above email either.

Thanks.

March 24 / From Hester,

Thanks! I did not receive that email in my inbox or my spam. Weird.

March 24 / From Hester,

This is so frickin' weird!! I checked all my email accounts and I rechecked the emails we shared and there are no attached documents or files. I will reach out to a classmate. Unfortunately, I don't have any of their contact info as I was absent the last time you may have asked for it. Do you have anyone's email I could reach out to?

March 24 / Hello, Hester,

What's weirder is that I emailed you the phone numbers and email addresses of all five members of your group because all of you will be "talking" to one another in those two mediums in early April.

Are you saying that you didn't get any of that, either?

Here are two of them (attached) so that you can call both and get everything you need, including the email addresses and the phone numbers of all the other members of your group.

Collegially,

Bob Eidelberg

March 24 / From Hester,

Thank you so much!! I have no idea what's happening. I receive some of your emails but some of them I don't have. Which of my email addresses are you mainly corresponding with?

March 24 / Hello, Hester,

Aha! And oops!

I've been mainly using the one you personally wrote down on the "Colleague Profile" form I gave you to fill out on your first day in the course.

Collegially,

Bob Eidelberg

April 7 / From Hester (to her groupmates),

Hey guys, I'll be sending my essay on "Eleanor Oliphant Is Completely Fine" tonight or tomorrow.

Thanks.

Hi Everyone (in the group),

My favorite (book) author, Martin Amis, endorses (poem) author Philip Larkin in his book "Philip Larkin: Poems Selected by Martin Amis." The "aging-as-waiting" poem I chose was "High Windows," which stood out to me most in terms of age and growth. It's not really about age, rather longing. What do we all wait for, want to return to? What do we take for granted? (I've attached it to this group email.)

End of April / From Hester on "the nature of time" – after reading the novel EINSTEIN'S DREAMS,

"Einstein's Dreams" the ~dreamy~ collection of fictional stories about time and space, written by Alan Lightman, is an odd and thought-provoking set of concepts. The nature of human relationships is a constant, whether humans spend a day of living together – existing in the space summer or winter – or everlasting, where suicide is suited for few. It seems humans always need one another, we seek companionship, friendship, love.

To put it bluntly, time is weird. The state of time that we exist in, day to day, our normal, is put into question. What would life look like if we didn't know what time was like? What if we aged backwards? Frankly, it's impossible to know. "Einstein's Dreams" is a fun read, but it romanticizes the concepts of time in flowing imagery, that is, at times, hard to get through. Friends meet up, on the dot, at twelve, having made tea plans. We wade through thick forests, flowery meadows, and the elderly sit in their wooden homes, retiring quietly into the night, dreaming of their colleagues' bagel brunch.

I don't think time works quite like that. I think time can be agony. Absolute agony. The only story that stuck with me, in a truthful manner, was one of the final pieces. A tale of terror. The widely worshipped Clock of Time. That sounds a lot more modern.

We live in fear of our age. Getting older. Women feel their biological clocks at twenty: "Have a baby! Use this anti-aging cream! Get Botox for your wrinkles!" Men feel it too, of course. Ticking. Waiting.

May 6 / From Hester – "a found poem" in Samuel Beckett's play WAITING FOR GODOT

A crust of bread
Beat him till he was dead

Where did you spend the night?
You better tell me

You piss better when I'm not there.
(They murmur)

This is awful!
(Another of your nightmares...)

Show me your leg, pull up your trousers.
Bloody radish

You're merciless! (The horror!!)

It's a turnip!

A carrot?
I could've sworn...
(A cretin. A halfwit! The slobber. A goiter!!)

You're making me nervous

Oh just get rid of him.

May 18 / Dear Mr. Eidelberg,

Hope you are healthy and doing well. I checked Blackboard and CUNYfirst online for my grade but I don't see it uploaded yet!

Thanks,

Hester

May 19 / Hello, You Five Colleagues,

I don't know who or what messed up, but my course grades (including six Incompletes) were "finally" posted at 10:40 last night, so don't WAIT to check them out.

Collegially,

Bob Eidelberg

Patrick is a senior who lives in the Bronx, New York, and commutes to Hunter College by subway (which he misses no opportunity to write about). Patrick is majoring in media studies, with a minor in creative writing. He plans on becoming either a filmmaker or a writer. Last fall, Patrick (along with current colleagues Valeria and Shanya) was in my other special topics English Department course on "The Teacher and Student in Literature." He earned an "A" because of his strong intellect, determined work ethic, and fine imagination. However, Patrick was most renown in that course for being able to sketch what was going on in our classroom while being himself completely attentive to and insightfully engaged in our class's lively discussions.

During the first half of "The Literature of Waiting" course Patrick continued to engage and be engaged (in his sketching): he even shared with me some ideas about possible design choices for our course's book SOME DAY: The Literature of Waiting. During the distance learning half of the course, Patrick's college work and home life were negatively impacted by serious health problems among several members of his immediate family. Yet, slowly and steadily Patrick saw that he would do all the required work and more, again earning an on-time final course grade of "A." What I would love to know, though, is whether he was able to find time to do any sketching.

Portrait of On-Campus Patrick

February 2 / Hello Professor,

Today's date is a palindrome! Apparently this is the first time in 909 years.

I guess humanity will be waiting for the next one!

Regards,

Patrick

February 13 / Hello Professor,

Hope you're having a fine afternoon! I could have sworn I passed my tutorial on "how to be a person who waits" forward last class session, but as I was going over the Coursepack, I found a copy of it inside. Not sure if this is a redundant copy, so below I have attached the tutorial, and I will bring a copy in to class tonight. I apologize for the inconvenience this may cause.

With warm regards,

Patrick

February 20 / Hello Professor,

I'm having a really bad bout of nausea, which is making it very hard to concentrate. I have attached my assignment below. I understand you may not see this message but I will let one of my classmates know, and hopefully they will catch me up on tonight's discussion.

P.S.: I saw one of the productions on YouTube of "The Dumb Waiter" and I am very eager to talk about it at some point.

Regards,

Patrick

February 25/ Hello Professor,

For some reason the delivery for my copy of the novel "Waiting" has not arrived in the mail. It says delivery was attempted but it has been about a week and a half. As such, I have not read the full novel. I bought the e-book, so as to not miss out on the discussion, but I don't think I'll be able to finish by tonight's class, or on time to do the assignment. I'm working on resolving the issue with the post office but I'm not sure what I can do about the assignment due tonight, as I have not yet read the full work.

Regards,

Patrick

February 27 / Hello Professor,

I know this isn't the promised correspondence about the BBC's production of "The Dumb Waiter," but thought it worth mentioning that Netflix actually made an adaptation of "The Haunting of Hill House," which goes very deep into the family's generational trauma dealing with living at Hill House. I haven't read the novel, so I don't know just how closely it follows the source material, but felt it was worth mentioning that it delved into a psychological aspect of sorts. I will draft an email tomorrow afternoon on my thoughts on the BBC production of "The Dumb Waiter" compared to my own reading of the text. Hope you have (or have had, depending on when you read this) a good night.

Regards,

Patrick

March 3 / Hello Professor,

I have flu-like symptoms right now. I was told by my father (who is a board certified physician and surgeon) that it would be best if I stayed home. My condition is improving, so I will likely be in class Thursday. I apologize for any inconvenience. I will contact a classmate to catch up on what was missed.

Regards,

Patrick

P.S.: I have attached the waiting journals below.

March 3 / Hello, Patrick,

Is there a doctor in the house? Yes, apparently. And you are wise to have taken his advice.

Hope to see you 100 percent better on Thursday.

Thanks for the three journal entries. Could you also email me by Wednesday night at the latest your top three choices for the independent reading, please?

Collegially,

Bob Eidelberg

March 4 / Hello again,

My choices for the independent reading are 1. The Haunting of House, 2. The Age of Innocence, 3. Great Expectations. I would REALLY like to do it on "The Haunting of Hill House," but I understand If I was too late.

Regards,

Patrick

March 9 / Professor,

I apologize, as this is really late, but I just realized that my last email failed to send, meaning I thought I had reached out about not feeling fit for class, when I actually didn't. I realize this may be an inconvenience and I apologize sincerely. I will get what I missed from a classmate.

Regards,

Patrick

Portrait of Distance-Learner Patrick

March 22 / Hello Professor,

I'm not sure how, but it seems I don't have the handout you mentioned in your most recent Blackboard post. I also am not sure what writing assignment I am to hand in for "Waiting for the Barbarians."

Regards,

Patrick

I hope you are staying well and healthy.

March 24 / Hello Professor,

I do not have a pristine copy of the found poem, as I wrote it on my work computer and I am working from home. I can, in the next day or so, get to you a copy of it that I have retyped based on the evaluated copy you handed back.

Regards,

Patrick

I hope you are well.

March 24 / Hello again Professor,

I will certainly try to help with the art on SOME DAY (Shanya mentioned on the phone that you had shared that thought with her). Perhaps a meaningful symbol of "waiting" from one (or more) of our novels would fit as a symbol for our thinking and studying of the topic of waiting? Preferably one that aligns thematically and with your chosen colors of green on a yellow background.

Regards,

Patrick

I have also attached below my response to the prompts based on "Waiting for the Barbarians."

March 27 / Hello Professor,

Sorry to be emailing you with distressing news. My father was just tested positive for Covid-19, and the last 24 hours have been extremely rough. My family has been calling me for information I don't have, and I have been unable to focus on reading and doing assignments for my classes. My father is stable right now and currently self-isolating but it has been an extremely rough day to say the least and we are currently in information limbo. I was wondering if it would be okay for me to hand the rest of the work for this week in on Saturday or Sunday, which would give me enough time to catch up and get started on work for next week.

Regards,

Patrick

March 30 / Professor,

Thank you for your kind words. I will hand in what I can hopefully by tonight. I'm finishing up most of the work. I am slightly behind on my reading of "The Haunting of Hill House," however. I will hopefully finish by the 2nd.

Regards,

Patrick

March 31 / Hello Professor,

Sorry for the delay. I have attached my poem inspired by "Waiting for the Barbarians." I will also send some time tonight the waiting journal-inspired piece of creative writing.

My father is recovering well, although still very sick. I appreciate your leniency in the last few days.

Regards,

Patrick

March 31 / Hello again,

I have attached the creative assignment based on my quarantine waiting journal based on myself waiting for my neighbors to get the severity of the quarantine.

Regards,

Patrick

April 10 / Hello, Professor,

I appreciate how accommodating you have been to our class in this trying time. The reading and thinking assignments you've created to make up the distance learning half of our course have both been a light in this time. I hope that reading our completed assignments brings you a similar light.

Regards,

Patrick

P.S.: About the group members' responses, nobody responded to my work, and I was a little confused about what to do next.

April 10 / Hello, Patrick,

Thank you for your kind and "enlightening" words. Most certainly, reading and evaluating the class's usually quite extended responses to all my many academic and creative assignments is a full way to spend my time sheltered at home – but it has been, in fact, what has kept me totally sane (maybe that should read "what has totally kept me sane").

Glad to hear that your dad is recovering well, but what's this postscript about nobody responding to your work? That sounds like you're referring to your personal essay on the group reading of THE HAUNTING OF HILL HOUSE – yes? If so, nobody ever got that essay – including me – so please re-send it as soon as you can to all of us.

Collegially,

Bob Eidelberg

April 11 / Hello, Professor

Oh, there was an email chain where they were sending and I replied there multiple times. I've attached the essay along with the email chain.

April 11 / Hello to all in the Hill House group,

I have attached my essay below. I'll respond to one of yours tonight. I apologize for the delayed response, I have been dealing with family matters.

Regards,

Patrick

April 11 / Hello, Patrick, and help!

I see the top of the essay, but nothing I do enables me to access it in full. Please send it to me as a separate pdf.

Thanks.

Collegially,

Bob Eidelberg

April 15 / Hello Professor,

If you click on the pdf attachment it should open. Maybe right click it and try downloading it? I can try sending it as a link but not sure if that would help. Sorry for the delayed response, for some reason I did not get your reply, only when I went to reply again did I see that you had responded.

Regards,

Patrick

April 21 / Hello Professor,

I am going to send a few more things either tonight or tomorrow morning. I am sorry for so many late works, I am catching up on work currently. My father is now back to work and healthy, but my mom got sick and she's immunocompromised, so it has been a rough couple of days. My brother is also sick, and I live in the same house with him, so I've had to take extra precautions as well as assume his care. He has recovered enough to do some tasks on his own, so I finally have a little time to catch up on work. I saw the email about the extra credit, would I still be able to hand in the work I've missed? I attached tonight's homework as a word document, as well as a pdf. I hope that this solves any potential issue that comes up.

Regards,

Patrick

May 7 / Hello Professor,

I am currently finishing some of the assignments due for your class, but I seemingly won't be able to finish in time to submit them. I will likely have the extra credit assignments due tonight, though. I was wondering if it would be in my best interest to try and pursue an incomplete like you mentioned in your Blackboard announcement?

Regards,

Patrick

May 7 / Hello Professor,

Below I have attached extra credit assignment choice number 9. I will attempt to finish some of the other assignments by tonight.

Regards,

Patrick

May 7 / Hello Professor,

I have attached a writing I did inspired by my own pocket of frozen time. Inspired, of course, by Alan Lightman's novel "Einstein's Dreams."

Regards,

Patrick

May 7 / Hello,

I've attached another extra credit assignment. I apologize for the barrage of emails, I am currently finishing up work from all of my classes.

Regards,

Patrick

May 10 / Hello again Professor,

I have attached below my signed consent form for our course's book SOME DAY. Please let me know if you have trouble opening it.

P.S.: As you requested, I am working on an extra credit essay on the BBC production of "The Dumb Waiter," which I had seen on YouTube back in February and never got to talk to you about. As well as the one about "Groundhog Day."

May 10 / Hello again,

I am sorry for the delay, I had to re-watch the production and gather my thoughts on it. The production I saw on YouTube was this one:

196

https://www.youtube.com/watch?v=yYV0sbzElJQ&t=271s

Regards,

Patrick

May 10 / Hello Professor,

I have attached below the "Groundhog Day" assignment. I actually had a bit of trouble writing this one. As a possible future filmmaker, I was trying to stop myself from solely talking about the technical aspects of the film.

Regards,

Patrick

Wait for it: Patrick's End-of-Course Thoughts on Being an On-Campus Student of Waiting and a Distance-Learner Student of Waiting

Throughout this course, my idea of waiting has not changed. The course has, in an indirect way, shaped how I think about my waiting. Throughout the length of this course, waiting has been a constant, sometimes overwhelming weight to bear. In the first part of the course, it was waiting eagerly to be able to discuss the readings, while also being patient enough to let my classmates who rarely spoke have the opportunity to share their thoughts. Often the end result of that waiting would be that someone shared a similar thought about the reading and I was unable to share my thoughts the way I wanted. Those moments did not leave me disappointed, though. They were reaffirming and made me wonder why it was that we shared such similar ideas. Was it some shared experience we had as students? The experience of being in the same age group, perhaps? Or maybe the universality of the experience of waiting just calls out all these mutual experiences.

I would like to think that the important thing about the latter half of this course, despite being at home and quite a lot less interactive than it was before, is that it has given us all another shared waiting experience. This experience will be something we can agree about or disagree about and have lengthy discussions about once this is all over. This time has been stressful, and rife with seemingly endless bouts of monotonous, often anxiety-ridden waiting. Because of this, and the nature of waiting, it seems like all we can do is hope for the best and do our part. Ironically for me, I have been unable to fully put my effort into my classes due to the physical and mental health of my family. I am assured, though, by the idea that somewhere there are people waiting for the world to move on from this situation, just like our classmates.

Thinking and reading about waiting has been a welcome, although sometimes sobering, experience during this extremely stressful time. It has been a distraction at times and, at others, a reminder of just how shared the emotions about this pandemic really are. I truly do hope my classmates share this sentiment and have gotten some opportunity through the literature we've studied in and out of the class to reflect on the notion that waiting is something that, in the end, brings us together. We're all in constant states of waiting, much like the characters from every piece of literature we have gone over, and that's something that we'll still share.

Anne-Lilja (pronounced "Anna Lilya") is a lower junior majoring in psychology and minoring in both English and physics. She lives in Manhattan and commutes to Hunter by subway. Famous in our class for her almost calligraphic printing of all her homework (shared in group evaluations and paired evaluations of colleagues' creative writing), Anne-Lilja was running a high "A" in "The Literature of Waiting" course at its mid-point – and then the coronavirus struck and we all got furloughed into distance learning.

Anne-Lilja had on-and-off problems adjusting to remote learning and for long stretches stopped doing any of the course's required reading and writing. Her first comeback was around the time of the collegial group work on the contemporary novel ELEANOR OLIPHANT IS COMPLETELY FINE (mentally the title character is far from fine).

Still, Anne-Lilja needed to request that an Incomplete grade be entered for her on May 11 so that she could have the next several weeks to complete the course on her own, which she did by submitting early in June all fourteen of her missing academic writing and creative writing assignments (all based on the literature under study), as well as several extra creative projects. Anne-Lilja was back to being a solid "A" student.

Portrait of On-Campus Anne-Lilja

In response to the early impact of the coronavirus pandemic on our now completely off-campus student body, certain members of the administration of Hunter College emailed a communication to their faculty with the advisement that they notify students of Hunter's online counseling services and encourage those we thought might be in need. I immediately forwarded that email to about a third of my class.

April 3 / Hello, Colleagues,

Don't be hesitant to contact them if you are in need (see "Counseling for Students" email below).

Collegially,

Bob Eidelberg

Begin forwarded message:

Subject: Counseling for students
Date: April 3, 2020 at 8:44:27 AM EDT

As the pandemic continues, more people are experiencing the loss of loved ones. Some of these people are our students — some of you may already have heard from students whose relatives have died. It goes without saying that we should all treat them with sensitivity, flexibility, and consideration.

There is counseling available to students who want it. Counseling and Wellness Services is operating remotely at this time. Please encourage students to call their main number at 212.772.4931 to set up an appointment when they are ready. They are checking voicemail remotely and are responding to students within the business day. Students should also feel free to email them at personalcounseling@hunter.cuny.edu. The first step in their process is to schedule a phone meeting, which is typically scheduled within a day of a student's first outreach to them.

April 14 / Hi guys,

I hope you're all doing well and staying safe. I apologize for this being so late. I also needed to take some time off for mental health issues, in addition to responsibilities at home. Here's my essay.

Best,

Anne-Lilja

April 14 / Hello from Professor Eidelberg,

Thanks, Anne-Lilja. Worth waiting for: well-argued from an important perspective, and well-written.

And welcome back!

Collegially,

Bob Eidelberg

Rabeya is a lower senior. Born in Bangladesh, Rabeya came to United States in 2003 and currently lives in Manhattan, a relatively short subway ride from Hunter. Rabeya is majoring in medical lab science, minoring in English, and has as her career goal is to be a medical lab scientist or a genetic counselor.

Rabeya was coming into her own as a major contributor to our often intense class discussions about serious "waiting" literature when we all went remote and Rabeya found she had to overcome stressful family health issues while working to not fall behind in her reading and writing. Despite migraines, she more than succeeded, becoming one of the handful of students in the course who earned a final grade of "A+." It had to have made her mother very happy.

Portrait of On-Campus Rabeya

January 28 / Good evening,

I am in your English 25416 class from earlier today. I just had two things to say that I haven't been able to really say in class:

1) With regards to the quote: "We all fear when we are in waiting rooms. Yet we all must pass beyond them...," we've spoken about multiple interpretations of what it means. In addition to what was discussed, I think that when it comes to this fear that's mentioned, it's not only in anticipation for what is to come, but also the fear of wasting time/ losing time from unnecessary waiting. This first half reminded me of my personal annoyance with literal waiting rooms where I tend to get antsy thinking about how much longer I'll have to wait when I have many other tasks and obligations at hand. Especially as a New Yorker, time is very valuable and everyone is rushing about. Waiting rooms not only exercise our patience, but also make us worry about losing time that can be used to do something else INSTEAD of waiting for something else to happen. Nonetheless, more often than not, we are required to face the fear and sit through waiting periods to finish the present task and move onto the next ("the beyond").

2) If the children's book "Waiting Is Not Easy!" was titled "Waiting Is Hard!," it would convey a pretty different attitude towards waiting. The title "Waiting is not Easy!" depicts a hopeful attitude towards the concept of waiting–that although it's not easy, it is doable. Meanwhile, the title "Waiting is Hard!" has a more whining tone to it. It's as if the author/ narrator is complaining about waiting and dreads it.

I am looking forward to what the semester holds!

Thank you!

Rabeya

January 30 / Good morning,

I was thinking about our class discussion after class and forgot to send you a ONE MORE THING when I got home. Here it is:

Ben's anxiety in this play is manifested in his specificity and need for control over certain things. His "OCD" and specificity regarding small instructions and details depict his need for control and order. Even though he seems much more composed than Gus, who keeps moving around and asking lots of nervous questions, internally, he is worried about things potentially going wrong. His rather calm composure is just a façade for what's truly going on inside of him. Even his interest in the newspaper is a way of distracting himself as a form of escapism There is never 100% guarantee that their job will go as planned and it is at the order of their boss. If he cannot control that aspect of what he does or who he kills, he can at least try to control other variables in his life.

Thank you!

Rabeya

February 25 / Good morning,

I hope you are doing well. I was absent from class yesterday because of an unexpected doctor's appointment that I could not reschedule because the next available was in May. The appointment was at 3 pm (doctor ran late) and I had to miss my 3-hour microbiology lab in the Medical Lab Science Program at Brookdale. We were starting our individual lab project worth half our lab grade and I was mandated to attend the evening makeup class. That being said, I had to miss this class to balance everything out. It was a rush of events and coordinating with two other professors and the lab technician to make things work out. I am truly sorry for not being able to attend your class.

Instead of waiting until Thursday to hand in the creative writing assignment, I typed up my previously handwritten assignment and attached it to this email. I really hope you don't penalize for the lateness. Thank you so much!

Best,

Rabeya

P.S.: I just saw your reply to my previous one more thing. I have been overwhelmed balancing full-time school and three part time jobs that I am yet to answer your ONE MORE THING follow-up questions. I will try to get back to them before tomorrow's class.

February 25 / Good afternoon,

I'm truly sorry for being so last minute but I absolutely cannot make it to class today. I have been having awful period cramps the past few months and today's one of them. I have been waiting the day out to see if it gets better and if I can manage to come to class but I really cannot. I've been in bed all day and my laptop is dead from last night. I'll get the assignments in to you soon somehow. Thank you.

Sincerely,

Rabeya

March 13 / Good evening,

I hope you're well, Professor. Attached is the vignette assignment on "Waiting for Lefty" (which I had hand written for submission but class was obviously canceled and I had to type up to email you) and the answers to the 2/4 sets of questions posted on Blackboard as per your instructions. Thank you!

Rabeya

March 17 / Hello, Colleagues,

A brief but really important message: if you currently do not have the email address of each and every other member of your independent reading group, please email me right away to get those email addresses you are missing.

In the next three weeks, not only will everyone in a group (and that's everyone!) be in direct contact with all their other group members as part of a soon-to-be-announced newly devised way for "oral communication" to again be a part of your independent reading assignment but also at least one other activity in our coursework before the end of the semester will require all group members to be in regular email contact and, perhaps, telephone/cellphone contact, with one another.

Start to think of your 5-person group as a mini-off-campus class in THE LITERATURE OF WAITING – one that I will also be involved in. Details to follow on the next several Blackboard announcements, so don't delay getting from me any contact information you are missing.

Collegially,

Bob Eidelberg

March 17 / Good evening,

I don't have anyone's contact info and don't really have a preference for particular people. I'd really appreciate if you could send me contact of some people to work with. Thank you!

Rabeya

March 19 / Good evening,

Attached are my answers to the reading questions. Thank you!

Best,

Rabeya

March 27 / Good evening,

Attached is my Session 17 assignment. I have been having awful migraines and this was the soonest I could get this assignment to you. It's meant to be submitted by Thursday night, and since technically Friday morning sunrise hasn't come yet (waiting ...), I hope this still counts as same-day submission.

Thank you!

Truly,

Rabeya

March 30 / Hello,

Attached is the pdf to the hw that is due tomorrow night. Thank you!

Rabeya

April 2 / Good afternoon Professor,

I am so sorry but I cannot submit my paper/response by tonight. My mom has been sick and it looks like she has coronavirus. I have been occupied with family responsibilities and could not finish the book I was assigned. She is on her way to the hospital and I am about to start disinfecting the entire apartment. I still have a small portion left to complete the assignment. If I can get a day or two extension without penalty, I'd much appreciate it. I'm so sorry.

Truly,

Rabeya

April 7 / Hello,

Attached is my reading response to ROSENCRANTZ AND GUILDENSTERN ARE DEAD. Thank you so much for allowing me to submit it at a later time and date and for being so understanding of my situation. I had finished it over the weekend and decided to hold on to the paper until today so that I can submit it with the follow-up assignment due (peer response to someone else's writing). Unfortunately, I don't think that is possible. My group members and I have a group text in which no one has been active on recently and no response yet to my message about exchanging our papers.

I will continue to **wait**. Unless they respond to the group text some time later today, I have no writing to respond to. In that case, the only other option would be if you can possibly send one of their assignments? I don't know.

Thank you!

Truly,

Rabeya

P.S.: The waiting journal-based creative writing assignment is due this week right? In that case, I will have it be emailed to you within a day or two.

April 8 / Hello, Professor

Thank you for sending it! Attached. Ryan and Jason already exchanged between themselves for the assignment via the group chat later In the day.

Rabeya

April 11 / Hello,

Attached are my waiting journals and creative writing piece.

Thank you!

Rabeya

April 13 / Hello,

Attached is my homework assignment due tomorrow. Thank you!

Truly,

Rabeya

April 19 / Good evening Professor,

I'd much appreciate confirming that I have received it.

ALSO, I'd much appreciate it if you'd kindly let me know where I currently stand in the course to best assess what step to take. Thank you!

Truly,

Rabeya

April 19 / Hello, Rabeya,

Through Session #22, you're a solid "A," Rabeya.

Collegially,

Bob Eidelberg

April 23 / Hey from Natalie (groupmate),

Attached is my poem.

Hope everybody is doing alright!

Nathalie

April 23 / Hi everyone,

Hope everyone's well. Attached is my assignment as per professor's instructions. Thank you.

Rabeya

May 6 / Hello, Colleagues,

Please address both of the two items in the very important large-type email below on (1) returning COURSEPACK to Mr.Eidelberg and on (2) getting your signed CONSENT FORM to him, the latter of which many of you have already done (and thanks!).

Also, if you are still thinking you might want to take an "incomplete" when I enter final course grades next week, you need to contact me RIGHT AWAY, if you have not yet made those arrangements.

Collegially,

Bob Eidelberg

May 7 / Hello Professor,

Thank you so much for such a wonderful class! I truly enjoyed it and am thankful for the experience even though we couldn't finish it in person. Attached is my final assignment. I hope you are well and that you stay happy and healthy.

Truly,

Rabeya

May 18 / Hello, Colleagues,

I delayed until today any official posting of final letter grades because of the great many Incompletes, but in fairness to those of you eager to learn what grade you earned already (truly earned!), I have now officially posted all grades including the several remaining Incompletes (to be changed, of course, at a later – but not too later from now – time).

Well done considering we were all alone together!

Collegially,

Bob Eidelberg

May 18 / Hello Professor,

I was just on the Blackboard page to see if you had posted any grades yet and remembered the permission slip we were all told to sign and complete. It totally flew past me with Ramadan, unable to print, and waiting for my laptop pen tip replacement to do it digitally. I am so sorry. I scrolled down to one of the older posts and saw that you had said to email it to you by May 10. Today is May 18, and I know it is plenty overdue but I thought I would sign and send it to you anyways. I'd rather know I tried than to just let it be and simply wonder what if. You'll find a digitally signed permission slip screenshot attached. What you decide is up to you and I'll respect it. Thank you!

Rabeya

May 18 / Hello Professor,

I don't see my grade on CUNYfirst or on Blackboard. Is this an error or are others unable to see it too? Thank you!

Truly,

Rabeya

May 18 / Hello Rabeya,

Thanks, Rabeya; you did right to send it even this late; I got it just in time to send it off to the publisher, who needed it by tonight.

Collegially,

Bob Eidelberg

May 19 / Hello, Rabeya and Her Four Colleagues,

I don't know who or what messed up, but my course grades (including six Incompletes) were "finally" posted at 10:40 last night, so don't WAIT to check them out.

Collegially,

Bob Eidelberg

Trever (with an "er") is an upper freshman from Bay Shore, New York, who currently resides (his "defacto address") in a Hunter College dormitory in Manhattan. Trever is majoring in English and minoring in philosophy, and wants as a career to be either a writer or an English teacher (and in class often wore both hats).

Had Trever's classmate and colleague – the graduating senior Ryan – had the opportunity to see more of Trever's creative writing (not all that possible during our distance learning phase), Ryan would have recognized one of his main competitors for the honor of best creative writer in the class. Trever also, in his in-class comments and his analytical at-home writing, demonstrated an impressive (particularly for a freshman!) knowledge of the humanities; it was a loss to the class that so many of Trevor's insightful ideas wound up only being seen by my eyes and pondered by my mind. Not surprisingly, Trever was one of the handful of students who earned a final letter grade of "A+" in the course (and he was definitely the youngest).

February 5 / Hi Prof. Eidelberg,

Portrait of On-Campus Trever

I'm sorry I missed class yesterday. I woke up with a bad stomach virus and needed to go to the emergency room because I'd regurgitated my medications I take every morning. Due to these circumstances I didn't get a chance to write in the waiting journal, but there certainly was a lot of waiting involved: waiting until I vomited again, waiting to be put in a bed, waiting for the nurse to come, waiting to feel better, waiting to be discharged ....

Anyway, I should be in class tomorrow.

Apologies,

Trever

Portrait of Distance-Learner Trever

March 25 / Hi Prof. Eidelberg,

I wanted to make sure you got the Kate Croy found poem when I sent it. I got a message saying there was some sort of spam filter and then you never acknowledged anything, so I wanted to check in to see if you got it or not.

Yours,

Trever

March 31 / Hello, Selected Colleagues,

This email may look like a duplicate of one of the ones I've sent out recently, but actually it is a new and very specific request asking that you put onto a clickable pdf (if you can) the first-rate creative piece of writing you did a while back inspired by one of your entries in your personal waiting journal.

I have read, evaluated, and graded (quite highly) the originals you submitted around the 9th and 10th of March, but in order for me to use these terrific pieces of writing in our course's book SOME DAY, I must have them re-sent to me on a pdf by no later than Sunday, April 5 (if humanly possible!). In any case, please respond to this email acknowledging that you have received this request of mine. Many thanks.

Be well, stay calm, be kind, stay sane.

Collegially,

Bob Eidelberg

March 31 / Hi Prof. Eidelberg,

I've attached the work for this past session. I also have a question I've been meaning to ask regarding the waiting journal creative writing assignments. You may have noticed that my past one was about a child, but still involved

212

waiting. It was inspired by when I saw a kid enter the subway station by himself while I was waiting for the train. I meant to ask, but I kept forgetting to: do the stories themselves have to also be about waiting? Or about our waiting experience?

Thanks,

Trever

PS: I'm going to send the assignments you asked for now, in responses to the individual emails.

April 2 / Hi everyone in the ROSENCRANTZ AND GUILDENSTERN ARE DEAD group,

Not sure if these are all the email addresses everyone uses but these are the ones I have. Here's my essay for the book SOME DAY.

Yours,

Trever

April 8 / Hi Prof. Eidelberg,

Here's my second journal-inspired piece. I'd like to have written a story, but I was having a hard time getting one out of what I had, so I went with more of a prose-poem instead.

Yours,

Trever

April 21 / Hi Prof. Eidelberg,

My thoughts on the three "Merrily We Roll Along" songs:

"Hills of Tomorrow": Basically reiterates the old "the sky's the limit" cliché.

"Our Time": Frank et al. express the idealism of their era, the countercultural era when young people thought they could change the world all by themselves.

"Merrily We Roll Along (1964-1962)": Similar to "Our Time," the song reflects idealism of youth, but in this case emphasizes that dreams take time to realize.

Yours,

Trever

April 22 / Hi everyone in the group,

The poem that most came to mind for me was "The Love Song of J. Alfred Prufrock." It's not about waiting, on the surface, but it touches on the idea that all of life is waiting, both waiting in general and waiting, specifically, to die. There's also a lot of time-related language; the "time for you and time for me" reminded me a little bit even of "Merrily We Roll Along," although the line isn't representative of the poem as a whole.

https://www.poetryfoundation.org/poetrymagazine/poems/44212/the-love-song-of-j-alfred-prufrock

Trever

P.S.: Sorry I used this, because it's a bit long, but it's what came to mind.

April 29 / Hi Prof. Eidelberg,

Sorry this is a day late, my fault.

The dream from 2 June 1905 in Alan Lightman's novel "Einstein's Dreams" really struck me. At first it seemed a bit silly, talking about the peach, but when the passage got to the woman and her husband aging in reverse, and later the man burying his friend, it became quite impactful to me. Death is one topic that almost never fails to make me emotional and contemplative, and the idea of death being undone, aging in reverse, was very poetic. Time in general makes me sensitive (for lack of a better word), so a lot of these passages were interesting to me, but this one in particular stood out. Aside from the poetic-ness of it, I began wondering as I read it how exactly this system was working. Was it only applying to some people, or to everyone? For the couple it seemed to apply to both of them, but it's unclear if the man burying his friend is also aging backwards. Also, how can time go backwards if things are still progressing? Do they go back every 24 hours? Because if you were to simply reverse time, we would just act like we were on a tape being rewound.

April 29 / From Trever on THE ICEMAN COMETH,

"A comparison of O'Neill to Beckett is hardly fair, since Beckett is infinitely the better artist, subtler mind, and finer stylist. Beckett writes apocalyptic farce, or tragicomedy raised to its greater eminence." – Scholar Harold Bloom in a 2006 foreword to THE ICEMAN COMETH published by Yale University Press

I planned on reading "The Iceman Cometh" for extra credit, but after reading the list of characters I decided it's probably better to watch rather than read, and I haven't gotten around to it yet. However, I have a general idea of the attitude Bloom attributes to O'Neill and how it contrasts to Beckett's. The world Beckett creates moves beyond the desperation a lot of other authors of modernity and post-modernity have depicted, and is a realm of resignation to the bleak world that is. It's quite a feat, really, and although people have tried to capture a type of secular, unfixable emptiness (Bret Easton Ellis, for example), no one's been able to do it the way Beckett has.

May 2 / From Trever on WAITING FOR GODOT,

I've read this play once before; it was a while ago, but I do have some pre-understanding. I've also read some other Beckett, so not to brag, but I do have a bit of familiarity with Beckett's style and worldview.

Questions I found myself asking while reading the play:

* Where was Vladimir?
* What are they suffering for?
* Why did Estragon sleep in a ditch?

* Why did Estragon get beat up?
* What does Vladimir "feel...coming on"?
* Why are they waiting for Godot?
* What is the relationship between Estragon and Vladimir?
* Why do they consider hanging themselves to pass time so casually?
* Why and how did they "[give up their] rights"?
* What is the cry?
* Who is Pozzo?
* Is Lucky a human? If so, why is he treated like a pack mule?
* Why does Pozzo break down over having had a slave so long?
* Why can Lucky only think with his hat on?
* Is there any actual meaning to what Lucky says?
* Why do they keep looking inside of the hats?
* Did Estragon attempt suicide? (Based on reference to having jumped in the Rhone once.)
* What is the significance of Estragon's boots? (And on a related note, the bowler hats?)
* Who is beating Vladimir and Estragon?
* If they used to live in France (I looked up what Macon country is), where are they now? Google says that "Cackon country" was a play on "caca," that is, shit, but where is it?
* Why the recurring use of "pig" as an address?
* Why does Vladimir keep singing?
* Who did Estragon see coming that they had to hide?
* Why was "critic" the worst insult?
* What's wrong with Pozzo?
* Why does Estragon use Abel as his first guess (and logically then Cain as his next guess for Lucky's name)?
* Why does Estragon hurt his foot again? What's the significance (especially given the motif of his boots)?
* Who really is Godot? What does he represent (since he doesn't seem to actually be providing any service of value to Vladimir and Estragon)?

Shanya is an upper junior who commutes to Hunter College by subway from her home in downtown Brooklyn, New York. Shanya is majoring in biology, minoring in both English and psychology, and plans on becoming a cardiothoracic surgeon. Shanya has one of the tiniest (and neatest) printing penmanships I have ever read; I CAN read it, though, and have done so with a good deal of pleasure throughout the two special topics English Department courses that Shanya has taken with me – The Teacher and Student in Literature and The Literature of Waiting.

Shanya's printing may be miniscule but the critical thinking and creativity she expresses in her writing is huge. This semester, once we devolved into distance learning, Shanya's writing – both academic and creative – had to go into pdf mode (it had always been "pdf" in the sense of "pretty darn fantastic") and, not surprisingly, many of those pdfs wound up being featured in our course's book SOME DAY: The Literature of Waiting.

Shanya received an A+ from me in both of my special topics courses, and she has taken it upon herself as a personal homework assignment to come up with a third special topics course for me to teach before she graduates next year. But with one caveat: not online, not by remote control. Like me, Shanya is not a big fan – in large part because we are such fans of each other as actual colleagues, as students of the kind of teaching and learning that can only truly take place in intimate, diverse, spontaneous, unpredictable campus classrooms.

Portrait of On-Campus Shanya

January 29 / Good Afternoon Professor Eidelberg,

First I'd just like to say how awesome it was to be back in your classroom yesterday with my former (and current colleague) Patrick! It was something I truly waited for and heavily anticipated over winter break. I was able to go through my Coursepack and I realized that I am missing three items:

The Odyssey excerpt
Waiting for Godot (commentary)
Passing Time (translated excerpts)

Collegially,

Shanya

February 14 / Good Evening Professor Eidelberg,

I am extremely sorry for missing today's class. I have attached my creative assignment that was due today as well. On Sunday, my family and I went out for our typical family dinner, but we tried a new restaurant and it didn't bode well. I came down with a bad case of food poisoning on Monday morning and I have been heavily medicated, in and out of sleep, unable to eat and trying to take in as much fluids as possible since then. I was hoping that I would be up to it by this evening, but I haven't been able to get out of bed and I am still in a great deal of pain. I am sorry for the late notice, as you can imagine, I have been kinda out of it and not myself. Is it possible that you could pass along Patrick's email so that I could catch up on everything that I missed today?

Also, I was planning on sharing this with you today. On Friday evening, my cousin Kila asked me to read with her and the book she chose was "Oh, the Places You'll Go!" by Dr. Seuss. In it, there is a mention of "The Waiting Place." It struck me almost immediately and I thought about everything we've discussed so far. I found her 7-year-old reaction to waiting to be very wise. She told me that every place was the waiting place because she waited everywhere she went and before everything that he did. She said "little kids live waiting lives because their parents control their time all of the time."

Collegially,

Shanya

Portrait of Distance-Learner Shanya

March 18 / Good Evening Professor Eidelberg,

This email is long overdue. In an effort to preserve the transparency in a relationship that I have come to value dearly, with a professor that I thoroughly enjoy, this week was by far one of the roughest weeks I've had thus far. On Monday, I woke up with no voice, a high fever and a really bad sore throat, I was unable to get out of the bed and just felt mentally and physically exhausted. I believe my sickness was brought on by the cumulation of a few sleepless nights, a ton of stress, and exposure to some pretty sick kids during my clinical volunteering. I have been bed-ridden since Monday, only finally able to get out of bed and move around the house Friday morning.

Despite having completed my reading in advance (both the handout copy and the physical book copy I own of "Waiting for Lefty," I had not yet completed my writing. While in bed on Monday, I produced many versions of the two creative assignments and they were horrible. Considering how dearly I value the course and your opinions on my writing, I refuse to turn in garbage so I resolved to rest and re-attempt the assignments when I was feeling better and my creative channels were less congested. The moment I felt just a little bit better, I got my assignments done. I have attached to this email:

- *"Waiting for Lefty" C.W. assignment,*
- *Personal Waiting Journal Entry C.W. assignment,*
- *Five Favorite Sentences from "A Telephone Call,"*
- *Responses to Prompts for "A Telephone Call" and for "Waiting For Lefty,"*
- *and my recommendations of four journal entries of my classmates' writing for our course book SOME DAY.*

I'm sorry for my lack of communication. But I am even more sorry that our course will be cheated of all the joy of our class discussions. Our class was the best part of my Tuesdays and Thursdays and I learned so much about myself as a reader, writer, and "waiter" from my colleagues – through their insights and their writing. While I have no doubt that you will find a way to make it work, I just wanted to recommend maybe trying Zoom, or Blackboard, as a platform for holding live classes where we could actively discuss with each other, whether through video camera or audio, or even a chat. I am willing to help in any way that I can. Also if it is possible, can you please email me the new calendar of sessions that you distributed on Tuesday.

I will have more writing for you by Sunday.

Collegially,

Shanya

March 16 / Good Evening (or Morning) Professor Eidelberg,

I have attached the responses to the questions regarding Session 14. I was wondering how the grading will work with the class being online. While the grades for each assignment are important to know, I'm more interested in the "in the margin" insights you regularly share on our work. Do you know yet how we will "get back" our graded assignments per se?

Will email the work for Session #15 by Thursday and will be checking the mail today and tomorrow looking for my freshly mailed and delivered calendar of sessions.

Side Note – Is it possible for you to email me Anne-Lilja's information? I haven't heard back from my colleagues (whose information that I have) whom I've contacted.

Collegially,

Shanya

March 16 / Good Afternoon Professor Eidelberg,

I just want to confirm, so we are emailing our written assignment (for the "Great Expectations" group) to you as well as the group. Are we to do anything with our group members' written assignments? Is there a required group aspect to the assignment?

Collegially,

Shanya

From: *Robert Eidelberg*
Sent: *Monday, March 16, 2020 3:49 PM*
To: *Shanya, Nattapat, Gabriella (and, of course, Massiel)*
Subject: *GREAT EXPECTATIONS GROUP'S CONTACT INFO*

Hello, Colleagues in Massiel's group,

Fyi to all four of you with "great expectations": contact information (see below) all of you will need for sharing your independent reading's written assignment with one another (as well as with me).

Collegially,

Bob Eidelberg

March 19 / Good Afternoon Professor Eidelberg,

I have attached my writing regarding "Waiting for the Barbarians" that was due today. Also just wanted to let you know that I reached out to my group and we are now all connected and communicating successfully.

In regards to our discussion about ideas regarding getting the work back to us, I am stumped. It is pretty hard for a course structured like ours. My creative writing professor is implementing an idea that will have us submit our writing on Blackboard as assignments and it gives her the ability to share her comments with us individually and give us a grade as well.

My mom has also created a Google classroom class for her class where they have discussions about reading via a discussion board, submit assignments, and she then provides them with annotated feedback and a grade on their writings pretty easily, as if she is reading and annotating with a pen and paper. Hopefully this information helps, and if not I am always here to help in any way that I can, especially to aid in this tough transition.

Also a couple of my classmates have asked me to reach out to see if you were still considering the possibility of holding online class sessions via websites like Zoom to increase our interaction and provide us the ability to engage in some sort of discussion with you and each other about the texts we read. I don't know why they reached out to me to ask, but I am more than happy to help.

Collegially,

Shanya

March 22 / Good Evening Professor Eidelberg,

I attached my found poem on Kate Croy ("The Wings of the Dove") to this email.

Collegially,

Shanya

March 24 / Good Afternoon Professor E,

I attached my "2030 Shanya to 2020 Shanya" letter in pdf form and my "How to Wait" tutorial in pdf form to this email. Thank you for considering me for publication in SOME DAY, and I will have some more writing for you in the coming days.

Collegially,

Shanya

March 25 / Good Afternoon Professor Eidelberg,

I just wanted to confirm if the work for Session 18 is still due on Tuesday, March 31st, because there is a lot of confusion after the CUNY-wide email regarding the Recalibration Period from 3/27 - 4/1. In their email they state that there is no distance learning classes to be held or assignments to be given during this period, so I just wanted to touch base so that we are all on the same page.

Thank you,

Shanya

March 26 / Good Afternoon Professor,

I have attached my Session 17 responses to "Waiting for the Barbarians." I hope to have my Session 18 work in by the end of the day, but will definitely have it in by March 31st.

Collegially,

Shanya

March 30 / Good Morning (or late evening) Professor Eidelberg,

I have attached (in pdf form) my responses to the Session #18 questions, my poem on "waiting," and a "one more thing" that I completed regarding the various covers I came across for the novel. Hopefully you can share your thoughts regarding the covers as well.

On a different note, I will have my signed consent form mailed off by Wednesday of this week. Also would it be possible for you to just check in with me regarding the quality of my work (after you read, and reread, my Session 18 work) or with some insights to my grade in the course? I am just a huge fan of receiving feedback so that I can change or maintain my approach to the work, especially in a class as collaborative (student and teacher) as ours was/is.

Collegially,

Shanya

P.S. I noticed that I have been sending my previous session work as Microsoft documents; if there are any that you need me to resend as pdfs, please let me know.

April 4 / Good Afternoon Professor Eidelberg,

I have had some ideas and planned in my schedule to get it done by this weekend. I can have it to you by Tuesday, if that's okay? I got hit with two exams for this weekend.

Collegially,

Shanya

From: Robert Eidelberg
Sent: Saturday, April 4, 2020 4:01:21 PM
To: Shanya
Subject: Growing Up?

Hello, Shanya,

My subject line is not a question I'm asking you about what you've been doing with your life these days (I know what you've been doing with your life these days!). Instead, I need you to refresh my memory: have you been working (or plan to work) on a piece of creative writing about how "growing up is a kind of waiting"? Something inspired, directly or indirectly, by your very positive reaction to the Russell Baker memoir GROWING UP?

April 8 / Good Morning Professor Eidelberg,

I tried my best to keep it brief, but it seems as though my 2 am brain is quite hyperactive. I have attached my creative assignment inspired by "Growing Up" as well as a copy of my email to Nattapat – both in click-on-the-icon pdf form.

Please stay healthy.

Collegially,

Shanya

April 14 / Good Evening Professor Eidelberg,

I attached my pdf of my responses to the prompts for today's session. I also attached the pdf of my creative writing piece inspired by one of my ten "waiting" journal entries, as well as the entry that inspired it. Please let me know if you need to see all 10 entries. My creative piece tapped into a very serious topic from my past and I appreciate the chance to share this and heal.

Collegially,

Shanya

April 16 / Good Evening Everyone in Our Group,

I have attached my letter as a pdf. Not surprisingly, I also picked the fourth story in "The Decameron" as my favorite. I hope everyone is staying healthy, mentally and physically, during this crazy "waiting" period.

Collegially,

Shanya

April 15 / Hello, Shanya,

Such a powerful piece and, of course, I completely understand how writing it and sharing it is a "healing." Let me ask, though, where does the sharing end — would you prefer that it not be published in our course's book SOME DAY?

Excellent work on the prompts as well. No need to send any of the other journal entries — not required.

And a question: I'm thinking of NOT having the class read Eugene O'Neill's play THE ICEMAN COMETH. The play works better on the stage than on the page (I've seen three superb productions in my lifetime, two of which are currently on YouTube, and several of the play's monologues (set pieces) are not the kinds of things that are uplifting in normal times — and, particularly in our current state of emotional depression thanks to the pandemic and to pandemic politics, I'm thinking that it would be insensitive of me to require that it be read with written prompts and without any human in-class engagement with it by all of us in an intimate space like a classroom.

I think you probably already have a copy: would you be good enough, if you can, to kind of skim it (and also read about the play a bit online) and let me know your thoughts. It might turn out that this particular play is not even a good choice for future editions of this course on waiting, even though it's all about waiting in the form of "pipe dreams" (the hopeless dreams of the down and out) and waiting for, well, death. (WAITING FOR GODOT should not be a problem, though.) If even glancing at this play puts you off based on what I just wrote, please pass on it and let me know that the iceman goeth.

Collegially,

Bob Eidelberg

April 16 / Good Evening Professor Eidelberg,

The sharing is endless – I am completely fine with you choosing do whatever you please with my work. I know it is always in good hands. I am attaching a copy of my letter regarding "The Decameron" and have emailed it to my groupmates as well. Is more group work coming? I actually enjoy the group communication, though Nattapat seems to be the most active communicator, along with myself, in our group.

You were right, I do have a copy of "The Iceman Cometh" and it happened to be one of the works that I was most excited for. I skimmed the first couple of pages and did some research and it is definitely a play that I would love to read in its entirety.

I'd love for you to share the superb YouTube versions so that I can watch them. I saw a couple of different ones when I was looking around. Is Kevin Spacey in one of those versions? This play definitely seems to be dark – especially given the current emotional climate – but I personally don't shy away from dark. I wouldn't mind it, but I understand that not everyone will necessarily feel the same way. From what I've gathered in my skimming, the play seems to be full of waiting and expecting and would fit wonderfully in our course. I am definitely open to it, and maybe if you didn't want to require it, you could make it extra credit? In the future sections of this course (and hopefully our own), I am advocating that "The Iceman" stayeth.

Collegially,

Shanya

P.S. My signed contract is in the mail, you should be receiving it next week.

April 21 / Good Evening Professor Eidelberg,

I am attaching my responses to the songs for "Merrily We Roll Along" in pdf form. Unfortunately my song writing skills have not panned out anything worthy of reading, so I have nothing to submit for the extra credit CW song assignment.

Two more things: for our extra credit last session I am considering Option 1 ("The Iceman Cometh") and Option 4 ("Living Is a Kind of Waiting to Die"). Also, is the assignment you posted in the course materials section of Blackboard for Tuesday, April 28th?

Collegially,

Shanya

April 23 / Good Morning Everyone in Our Group,

I have attached the pdf of my short "waiting" poem and a brief introduction. After the poem, I also shared a brief song that is very grounded in waiting as well. Consider it an honorable mention. I hope you all are staying healthy and safe.

Collegially,

Shanya

April 29 / Good Afternoon Professor Eidelberg,

I'm sorry this message comes to you later rather than sooner. I've been having computer troubles for the past two days and was finally able to connect with tech support this morning and figure it out. I am attaching in pdf form my CW/HW assignment for Session #25.

Also in regards to your other announcement, have you received my signed consent form in the mail? My address will remain the same going forward, so you can one day send my copy of SOME DAY to my home, the same one you mailed the calendar of sessions to.

Collegially,

Shanya

May 3 / Good Morning Professor Eidelberg,

I have attached in pdf form my Session #26 work for our first encounter with "Waiting for Godot."

Collegially,

Shanya

May 5 / Good Evening Professor Eidelberg,

I have attached, in pdf form, my responses to the prompts for Session #27.

Hope all is well.

Collegially,

Shanya

May 7 / Good Morning Professor Eidelberg,

I am attaching my creative piece for our final session. Feeling particularly inspired, for my extra credit piece I chose to do some more toying with "Waiting for Godot." I have attached both pieces in pdf form.

On another note, I have been both dreading and waiting for this moment (actually after my experience with this course, I'm realizing those two may be synonymous). I am tremendously sad that my time in your class has come to an end and next semester I will have to take my newfound talents to other courses and professors – unless, of course, you want to create another class? (It was more than worth asking.)

In all, I just want to say thank you. Thank you for renewing my love of literature, language and possibility. When I registered last semester for your course on "The Teacher and Student in Literature," I was riddled with anxiety from the amount of stress that was put on participation, in the course description alone – and after the first day I was definitely determined to drop the course. But your demeanor was so welcoming that it inspired me to want to prove something to myself – and I did!

*So I thank you, Professor E. Thank you for seeing something in me that I failed to find in myself for years – a voice. Before your class, I never participated. Not in middle school, not in high school, and definitely not in college. Despite having the grades, I never felt like I was good enough. Your classes push students in all the ways they need to be pushed. Not only do I participate freely now in **all** of my other classes, but I also am no longer afraid of my sometimes kooky thinking.*

Thank you for giving me the opportunity to express myself in all of our creative writing assignments (from both semesters). I was able to go beyond developing relationships with the literature, but I was also able to rekindle my relationship with writing as a form of thinking, self-expression, and healing. Rick Dadier, Sylvia Barrett, Frank McCourt, Manna & Lin, Pip, and even the Magistrate have all touched my life in different ways and will forever be imprinted in my memory. You provided me the foundation for a strong support system both in and out of the classroom. Between the characters in the literature we were studying and my classmates, you helped me foster meaningful and withstanding connections, which it turns out I needed more than I knew. Your class got me through both semesters and for that I am grateful.

One more thing. In the first letter that I wrote last semester (to a remarkable teacher), I wrote: "You were more than an English teacher; you were a friend and a mentor" – and that, Professor Eidelberg, you are. After much thought about all that we discussed and learned in our course last semester, I realized that while many students are vocal about the teachers and professors they consider to be remarkably bad (sorta like what I hear at Hunter all the time), not many talk about those who are remarkably good. Usually the remarkably good teachers get talked about years later, while students reminisce and come to the realization of the effects of remarkably good teachers on their lives. So I just wanted to let you know now while I have the opportunity. Thank you for being you. The best English professor I've ever had, an unknowing friend (plenty of days, I entered your classroom feeling at my lowest, or super stressed out, and whether it be with your humor or your excitement for what we were learning and thinking about that day, all of my worries and stress dissipated) and a mentor.

I hope to apply half of your teaching skills to my future surgical career (fingers crossed). Also my possible literary career. I'll definitely swing by to visit next semester and hopefully we can keep in touch.

Collegially,

Shanya

May 18 / Good Morning Professor Eidelberg,

I hope all is well. I was just hoping that you could re-share the name of one of the plays we anticipated seeing this semester. I know that "Waiting for Godot" was one of them, but I can't seem to find where I wrote down the name of the other.

Collegially,

Shanya Hopkins

May 18 / Good Afternoon Professor Eidelberg,

Thanks for CAROLINE, OR CHANGE as the name of the Broadway musical the class was going to see late in April. I will definitely go see it when Broadway reopens (in the fall, I hope).

Also, I will get to work right away on a third course for you to teach before I graduate. A Hunter humanities course based on your self-improvement critical thinking book PLAYING DETECTIVE definitely sounds like my type of course. I spent many of my days as a child reading detective novels and listening to my grandfather retell the ones he read once he was done. I think that would be absolutely amazing. I'm glad to hear you have been doing well and keeping busy. My family is doing great, we've been using this time to share some of our passions – one of mine being writing – and the reception has been amazing.

I can't wait to read and reread our course's collaborative book "SOME DAY: The Literature of Waiting." I have recommended your other humanities course – "The Teacher and Student in Literature" (that produced your other collaborative book STAYING AFTER SCHOOL, right?) – to many friends, but, ironically, also recommended that they wait if forced to take the class online. The course is simply too magical to be minimized.

Thank you,

Shanya

AUTHOR ROBERT EIDELBERG'S BOOKS WITH A BUILT-IN TEACHER

In addition to **Hey, Professor: An Experiment in Distance Learning**, all of the following "Books With a Built-In Teacher" by educator and author Robert Eidelberg are available through all online bookstores as well as from the author by contacting him at glamor62945@mypacks.net

Some Day: The Literature of Waiting – A Creative Writing Course With Time on Its Hands

"Who's There?" in Shakespeare's HAMLET – That Is the Question!

Stanza-Phobia: A Self-Improvement Approach to Bridging Any Disconnect Between You and Poetry by Understanding Just One Poem (Yes, One!) and Winding Up Not Only Learning the Process Involved but Coming to Love at Least a Few More Poems (and Maybe Poetry Itself)

Good Thinking: A Self-Improvement Approach to Getting Your Mind to Go from "Huh?" to "Hmm" to "Aha!"

Playing Detective: A Self-Improvement Approach to Becoming a More Mindful Thinker, Reader, and Writer By Solving Mysteries

Detectives: Stories for Thinking, Solving, and Writing

So You Think You Might Like to Teach: 29 Fictional Teachers (for Real!) Model How to Become and Remain a Successful Teacher

Staying After School: 19 Students (for Real!) Have the Next What-if Word on Remarkable Fictional Teachers and Their Often Challenging Classes (a collaborative book based on the Hunter College course "The Teacher and Student in Literature")

Julio: A Brooklyn Boy Plays Detective to Find His Missing Father (with John Carter)

ABOUT THE AUTHOR

A former journalist, Robert Eidelberg served thirty-two years as a secondary school teacher of English in the New York City public school system, nineteen and a half of those years as the chair of the English Department of William Cullen Bryant High School, a neighborhood high school in the borough of Queens, New York.

For several years after that he was an editorial and educational consultant at Amsco, a foundational school publications company; a community college and private college writing skills instructor; and a field supervisor and mentor in English education for the national Teaching Fellows Program on the campus of Brooklyn College of The City University of New York.

For the past twenty-one years, Mr. Eidelberg has been a college adjunct both in the School of Education at Hunter College of the City University of New York and in the English Department of Hunter College, where he teaches literature study and creative writing courses on "The Teacher and Student in Literature" and "The Literature of Waiting," both of which he expressly created for Hunter College undergraduate students.

Mr. Eidelberg is the author of ten educational "self-improvement" books, all of which feature "a built-in teacher" and two of which he collaborated on with his students in the special topics humanities courses he teaches at Hunter College on "The Teacher and Student in Literature" and on "The Literature of Waiting."

Robert Eidelberg lives in the historic Park Slope neighborhood of Brooklyn, New York, with his life partner of 47 years and their Whippet, Chandler (named, as was his predecessor, Marlowe, in honor of noir mystery writer Raymond Chandler).